# A student's guide to Analysing Corporate Reports

T43746

by Paul Robins

KAPLAN

PUBLISHING

British library cataloguing-in-publication data
A catalogue record for this book is available from the British Library.
Published by:
Kaplan Publishing UK
Unit 2 The Business Centre
Molly Millars Lane
Wokingham
Berkshire
RG41 2QZ

ISBN 978-0-85732-204-3

© Paul Robins

First edition published 2010

Printed and bound in Great Britain.

Acknowledgements

We are grateful to the Institute of Chartered Accountants in England and
Wales (ICAEW) and the Chartered Institute of Management Accountants
for their permission to reproduce past examination questions in this book.
Ownership of the copyright in these questions belongs to them.  The
answers are the author's.

# Contents

# Chapter 1

## Introduction

## 1 Objectives of the chapter

**Having read this chapter you should be able to:**

■ appreciate the problems that are inherent in analysing corporate reports

■ describe the contents of a typical corporate report

■ identify 'users' and their information needs

■ outline the technique employed in the interpretation of financial statements.

## 2 Context for the book

The purpose of corporate reports is to provide useful information about the reporting entity to those users who have legitimate rights to receive such information. Unfortunately the task of gathering useful information from published corporate reports is not an easy one. This is partly because published corporate reports can be quite complex to interpret – even for an expert. It is also made difficult by the fact that the information a particular user might legitimately expect to receive is not available from the financial statements. Furthermore, those entrusted with the preparation of corporate reports often have a vested interest in presenting the reports in a manner that is not totally objective. Anyone who seeks to interpret corporate reports needs to bear all these factors in mind.

This book is particularly directed at accountancy students who need to be able to demonstrate skills in the analysis of corporate reports for assessment purposes. In the experience of the author this is an issue that causes problems for accountancy students in examinations and other assignments. There are many examples of published reports of examiners from professional accountancy bodies that speak of poor performance in analysis questions. It is often because answers lack structure and underlying rationale. A key purpose of this book is to provide a structure that can be used as a basis for the development of a reasoned interpretation of corporate reports by students.

Whilst the primary focus of the book is for accountancy students, the book also seeks to be of benefit to non-specialists who need some understanding of what published corporate reports can (and just as importantly cannot) tell a user about corporate performance.

The book does not seek to describe the preparation of corporate reports in any detail. However in order establish a coherent framework for the interpretation of corporate reports it will be necessary to outline the components of a typical corporate report. It will also be necessary to consider which parts of the corporate report are likely to benefit which user group.

# 3 The contents of a typical corporate report

## 3.1 The initial non-financial section

This section would typically contain a statement by the chief executive or chairman, an overall operational review of the business, and some non-financial statistics. We will consider these components in more detail in Chapter 6 of this book but it is worth noting that in general this section of the report is subject to less detailed regulation than the financial section of the report (see 3.2 below). Therefore there is often scope for management bias here.

## 3.2 The financial section

This section contains the financial statements themselves. Unlike the initial section (see 3.1 above) the contents of this section are subject to detailed regulation and, in the case of large and listed companies, this section of the report is subject to external audit. The exact format of these statements depends on the type of company – we will discuss this issue in more detail in Chapter 2. However typically this section would be in five parts:

- a statement of financial position (sometimes referred to as a balance sheet)

- a statement of financial performance (referred to variously as a profit and loss account, an income statement, or a statement of comprehensive income)

- a statement of the change in the shareholders interest in the business (a statement of changes in equity)

- a statement showing the inflows and outflows of cash (a cash flow statement).

- various notes to the financial statements that explain the principles under which the financial statements have been prepared (the accounting policies) and give more detail on the summarised amounts that are included in the financial statements themselves (for example a breakdown of the total sales by geographical region).

It is this part of the corporate report that will usually be relied upon most by analysts.

## 4 Users and their information needs

### 4.1 Equity investors

Equity investors provide the 'risk capital' for an entity. They have no guaranteed return on their investment. Their investment is not 'repaid' by the entity and their normal exit route is to find a buyer for their investment. They need information on whether to keep their investment or whether to attempt to sell it, and potential investors need to receive information to assist them in deciding whether or not to invest in the 'risk capital' of an entity. They also need information to assess the ability of the entity to make a dividend payment to them (based on the profits the entity has made).

This user group will primarily be interested in the profits the entity has made, as this will be a key factor driving the dividend payment and the underlying value of the investment. This group will also be interested in the liquidity (or cash generating ability) of the entity as dividend payments are almost always made out of the cash resources of the entity.

Equity investors are often seen as the primary user group and the financial section of a corporate report is usually prepared with the information needs of this group as a primary focus. That said, other user groups are also likely to benefit from the information that is provided in the financial section of the corporate report.

### 4.2 Employees

From a financial perspective, employees will be primarily concerned with the remuneration they receive from the entity. This remuneration will partly be related to the current period (in the form of salary payments) and partly to the future (in the form of retirement benefits. They will also have the long term stability of the entity as a key focus as this will be directly relevant in evaluating their job security. Other non-financial factors (such as the working environment and the style of management) will also be of relevance to them.

The financial section of a corporate report is less 'user friendly' to the employees than it is to the equity investors. It regards employee remuneration as a 'cost' in the statement of financial performance and takes an 'entity focus' on the issue of the provision of retirement benefits. Nevertheless the long term profitability and short and long term liquidity of an entity is of some relevance in assessing their job security.

The non-financial section of a corporate report may well provide information that is of relevance to employees. For example some entities will provide a report in which they describe their employment policies and the extent to which they interact with the community in which the entity is located.

## 4.3 Lenders

For obvious reasons the primary concern of lenders will be whether their loans, and the interest attaching to them, will be paid when due. Therefore their primary financial focus will be on the ability of the entity to generate cash, and therefore on its liquidity.

## 4.4 Suppliers

There is some overlap between the information needs of suppliers and those of lenders. Suppliers will often have supplied the entity on credit, and so can be said to be 'short term lenders'. They will also be concerned with the longer term prospects of the entity as this will directly affect the likelihood of repeat business from the entity.

## 4.5 Customers

The information needs of customers overlap to some extent with the information needs of suppliers. Customers will have an interest in the continued ability of the entity to supply them with goods and services. This ability will be directly related to the longer term prospects of the entity.

## 4.6 Government and government agencies

The information needs of government and their agencies firstly concern the taxable capacity of the entity and its likely contribution to national income. They are also concerned more generally in the contribution of the entity to national statistics.

## 4.7 The public

In the environment in which the entity is located, the public will have a legitimate concern about the contribution the entity is making to the local economy, particularly in the field of employment. They will also be concerned about issues such as the impact of the entity's practices and policies on the local environment, for example whether the entity causes any kind of pollution by its processes.

## 5  Analysis of corporate reports – an outline of the technique

Analysis of corporate reports involves a scrutiny of the corporate report of a company (usually focusing on the financial statements) with a view to drawing conclusions about some aspect of its financial position or performance. It is difficult to assess whether financial analysis is 'correct' and, from a student's perspective, this makes it quite difficult to study.

A key factor to remember when performing financial analysis is that the numbers analysed are only useful when they are compared with something. If you were told that the sales revenue of a company for a period was £10 million you could not draw any meaningful conclusions from that information unless you knew more. You would be able to draw a more meaningful conclusion if you knew (for example) what the sales revenue of the company had been for an equivalent earlier period. What is required is some sort of yardstick of comparison. This yardstick could typically be one of the following:

■ an equivalent number for an earlier period

■ an equivalent number for another company for the same period

■ an equivalent 'industry average' for the same period

■ the relevant amount that had been budgeted for by the management of the company.

From a student's perspective the yardstick of comparison is inevitably based on the data that is provided in the relevant question. However it is important to be aware when drawing conclusions that we are comparing numbers that are actually comparable. If the numbers are not comparable, then the conclusions will be invalid. Factors that might limit the validity of comparison would include:

- the impact of inflation when, say, comparing this year's sales revenue to last year's

- the effect of differing business practices when comparing numbers from one company with those of another

- the 'size effect' – it would clearly be invalid to compare the sales revenues of a small local business with those of a multi-national.

It is in order to address the third of the above issues that 'ratio analysis' is widely used when analysing financial statements. As an example, we have said in the previous paragraph that a comparison of the sales revenue of companies of different sizes would clearly be invalid. However it might be perfectly valid to compare the ratio of profit to sales even where the companies are of totally different sizes. The technique is powerful, widely used, and will be described in detail in later chapters of this book.

It is important to sound a cautionary note to students here though: ratio analysis is more than just computing a ratio and saying it is greater or less than the comparison ratio! It is important to identify potential reasons why the ratio might have changed and to speculate on the potential implications of this for the company whose financial statements are being analysed. In the chapters that follow we will suggest possible reasons for changes in key ratios as we describe them.

## Chapter summary

The analysis of corporate reports is an inexact science that often causes problems to students when attempting this in examinations. Corporate reports contain both a financial and a non-financial section. The financial section tends to be more closely regulated than the non-financial section. Therefore analysts usually place more reliance on the financial section of the report. The type of analysis that is performed depends on the information needs of the user group, which can vary considerably from group to group. However all financial analysis involves comparing two financial amounts (often financial ratios) and seeking to explain the implications of any variation for the entity under consideration.

# Chapter 2

## The overall structure of financial statements

## 1 Objectives of the chapter

**Having read this chapter you should be able to:**

■ describe the individual statements that comprise the financial statements of an entity that are prepared under the international framework. In particular you should be able to appreciate whether each individual statement primarily provides information about:

  ■ financial position at a particular date

  ■ financial performance over a period

  ■ change in financial position over a period.

## 2 The overall context

It might be assumed that accountancy students should be familiar with the overall structure of financial statements on the basis of other, related, studies, for example accounts preparation. Whilst this certainly ought to be the case, in the experience of the author many do not seem to apply this knowledge in the context of an exercise involving the interpretation of financial statements. Therefore a reminder of the overall structure of financial statements, and how the various components fit together, is a useful starting point in considering interpretation techniques.

The overall structure of financial statements is heavily influenced by the regulatory environment that applies to the relevant entity. As far as entities incorporated in the United Kingdom (UK) are concerned, there are basically two relevant regulatory frameworks, depending on the type of entity.

### 2.1 The international framework

Entities preparing financial statements under this framework base the preparation of their financial statements on International Financial Reporting Standards (IFRS). UK law allows any entity incorporated in the UK to use this framework, but a consequence of European Union (EU) law is that UK entities that have shares and securities listed on a recognised stock exchange are required to use IFRS in the preparation of their consolidated financial statements (financial statements that incorporate their subsidiaries – other entities that they control).

## 2.2 The UK framework

Entities preparing financial statements under this framework base the preparation of their financial statements on the Accounting Regulations of the UK Companies Act (for the overall structure) and on UK Financial Reporting Standards (FRS) (for the detailed recognition and measurement rules). The UK framework is becoming increasingly aligned with the international framework and at the time of writing the UK standard setting authority is considering a mandatory extension of IFRS to a wider range of UK companies.

Chapter 1 has stated that the primary focus of this book is to equip accountancy students to answer questions involving the interpretation of financial statements that appear in professional accountancy assessments. To a large extent the major UK accountancy bodies have moved to an assessment regime that is based on the international framework rather than the UK framework so this is the framework that will be the focus of this chapter, and indeed the whole book.

Under the international framework the objective of financial statements is to provide information about the financial position, performance and changes in financial position of an entity that is useful to a wide range of users in making economic decisions. This objective is served by the inclusion of four primary financial statements in corporate reports:

- the statement of financial position (formerly referred to as the balance sheet)

- the statement of comprehensive income (this statement reports on financial performance, and is sometimes presented as two statements – see section 4 below)

- the statement of changes in equity (this statement reports on changes in financial position)

- the statement of cash flows (this statement reports on a particular change in financial position).

## 3 The statement of financial position

International Accounting Standard (IAS) 1 deals with the overall presentation of financial statements. IAS 1 requires that an entity presents a statement of financial position at the reporting date and, as a minimum, a comparative statement at the previous reporting date.

An appendix to IAS 1 gives an illustrative structure for financial statements and this illustrative structure shows the following for the statement of financial position.

|  | 31 Dec 20X7 | 31 Dec 20X6 |
|---|---|---|
| **ASSETS** | | |
| **Non-current assets** | | |
| Property, plant and equipment | 350,700 | 360,020 |
| Goodwill | 80,800 | 91,200 |
| Other intangible assets | 227,470 | 227,470 |
| Investments in associates | 100,150 | 110,770 |
| Available-for-sale financial assets | 142,500 | 156,000 |
| | 901,620 | 945,460 |
| **Current assets** | | |
| Inventories | 135,230 | 132,500 |
| Trade receivables | 91,600 | 110,800 |
| Other current assets | 25,650 | 12,540 |
| Cash and cash equivalents | 312,400 | 322,900 |
| | 564,880 | 578,740 |
| **Total assets** | 1,466,500 | 1,524,200 |
| **EQUITY AND LIABILITIES** | | |
| **Equity attributable to owners of the parent** | | |
| Share capital | 650,000 | 600,000 |
| Retained earnings | 243,500 | 161,700 |
| Other components of equity | 10,200 | 21,200 |
| | 903,700 | 782,900 |
| Non-controlling interests | 70,050 | 48,600 |
| **Total equity** | 973,750 | 831,500 |

| Non-current liabilities | | |
|---|---|---|
| Long-term borrowings | 120,000 | 160,000 |
| Deferred tax | 28,800 | 26,040 |
| Long term provisions | 28,850 | 52,240 |
| Total non-current liabilities | 177,650 | 238,280 |
| | | |
| **Current liabilities** | | |
| Trade and other payables | 115,100 | 187,620 |
| Short-term borrowings | 150,000 | 200,000 |
| Current portion of long-term borrowings | 10,000 | 20,000 |
| Current tax payable | 35,000 | 42,000 |
| Short-term provisions | 5,000 | 4,800 |
| **Total current liabilities** | 315,100 | 454,420 |
| **Total liabilities** | 492,750 | 692,700 |
| **Total equity and liabilities** | 1,466,500 | 1,524,200 |

The statement is effectively in three sections:

- assets – the resources of the business

- liabilities – the obligations of the business

- equity – the total assets less total liabilities of the business.

Assets and liabilities are described as either current or non-current. Current assets/liabilities are defined in IAS 1. Basically the definition says that they are:

- assets/liabilities that are expected to be realised/settled within the normal operating cycle of the entity

- assets/liabilities that are held primarily for the purposes of trading

- assets/liabilities that are expected to be realised/settled within twelve months of the reporting date

- other assets/liabilities are non-current.

The format given in the appendix to IAS 1 (and reproduced above) is not mandatory. However IAS 1 does require that certain items are recorded on the face of the statement and, in the vast majority of circumstances, that distinction is made between current and non-current items.

In practices entities sometimes divert from the prescribed format. For example, some UK entities that report under the international framework show assets less liabilities on one side of the statement, and equity on the other. This has very little impact, though, on the use of the statement for analysis purposes. From an examination perspective, the format given above tends to be widely used.

## 4 The statement of comprehensive income

This statement measures the financial performance of an entity and is effectively in two parts. As stated earlier, in some cases the statement is actually presented as two separate statements. The illustrative structure for the statement of comprehensive income as set out in the appendix to IAS 1 is set out below:

| | 20X7 | 20X6 |
|---|---|---|
| **Revenue** | 390,000 | 355,000 |
| Cost of sales | (245,000) | (230,000) |
| Gross profit | 145,000 | 125,000 |
| Other income | 20,667 | 11,300 |
| Distribution costs | (9,000) | (8,700) |
| Administrative expenses | (20,000) | (21,000) |
| Other expenses | (2,100) | (1,200) |
| Finance costs | (8,000) | (7,500) |
| Share of profits of associates | 35,100 | 30,100 |
| **Profit before tax** | 161,667 | 128,000 |
| Income tax expense | (40,417) | (32,000) |
| **Profit for the year from continuing operations** | 121,250 | 96,000 |
| Loss for the year from discontinued operations | - | (30,500) |
| **PROFIT FOR THE YEAR** | 121,250 | 65,500 |

| Other comprehensive income: | | |
|---|---:|---:|
| Exchange differences on translating foreign operations | 5,334 | 10,667 |
| Available-for-sale financial assets | (24,000) | 26,667 |
| Cash flow hedges | (667) | (4,000) |
| Gains on property revaluation | 933 | 3,367 |
| Actuarial gains (losses) on defined benefit pension plans | (667) | 1,333 |
| Share of other comprehensive income of associates | 400 | (700) |
| Income tax relating to components of other comprehensive income | 4,667 | (9,334) |
| **Other comprehensive income for the year, net of tax** | (14,000) | 28,000 |
| **TOTAL COMPREHENSIVE INCOME FOR THE YEAR** | 107,250 | 93,500 |
| Profit attributable to: | | |
| Owners of the parent | 97,000 | 52,400 |
| Non-controlling interests | 24,250 | 13,100 |
| | 121,250 | 65,500 |
| Total comprehensive income attributable to: | | |
| Owners of the parent | 85,800 | 74,800 |
| Non-controlling interests | 21,450 | 18,700 |
| | 107,250 | 93,500 |

As with the statement of financial position, the above format is not mandatory but there are certain minimum amounts that must be included on the face of the statement, rather than in the notes to the financial statements. In examinations this format does tend to be followed.

As already stated, the statement is very much in two parts. The first part of the statement shows the profit or loss for the year. The majority of gains and losses an entity makes are included in this part of the statement and under the international framework this part of the statement can be separated out and shown as an 'income statement'.

THE OVERALL STRUCTURE OF FINANCIAL STATEMENTS

The second part of the statement shows gains and losses arising in the period that are not reported as part of profit or loss ('other comprehensive income'). There is a lack of clear theoretical rationale for whether gains and losses are part of profit or loss or are shown as other comprehensive income. Individual IFRSs determine whether relevant gains and losses are in profit or other comprehensive income. This lack of clarity makes the assessment of financial performance somewhat complicated. Conventional profitability analysis (see chapter 3 for more detail) tends to focus on profit rather than total comprehensive income.

An alternative presentational approach outlined in IAS 1 is to split the performance statement into 2 parts as shown below (with the same basic data as already shown).

**Income statement for the year ended 31 December 20X7**

|  | 20X7 | 20X6 |
|---|---|---|
| **Revenue** | 390,000 | 355,000 |
| Cost of sales | (245,000) | (230,000) |
| Gross profit | 145,000 | 125,000 |
| Other income | 20,667 | 11,300 |
| Distribution costs | (9,000) | (8,700) |
| Administrative expenses | (20,000) | (21,000) |
| Other expenses | (2,100) | (1,200) |
| Finance costs | (8,000) | (7,500) |
| Share of profits of associates | 35,100 | 30,100 |
| **Profit before tax** | 161,667 | 128,000 |
| Income tax expense | (40,417) | (32,000) |
| **Profit for the year from continuing operations** | 121,250 | 96,000 |
| Loss for the year from discontinued operations | - | (30,500) |
| **PROFIT FOR THE YEAR** | 121,250 | 65,500 |
| Profit attributable to: |  |  |
| Owners of the parent | 97,000 | 52,400 |
| Non-controlling interests | 24,250 | 13,100 |
|  | 121,250 | 65,500 |

**Statement of comprehensive income for the year ended 31 December 20X7**

|  | 20X7 | 20X6 |
|---|---|---|
| **Profit for the year** | 121,250 | 65,500 |
| **Other comprehensive income:** | | |
| Exchange differences on translating foreign operations | 5,334 | 10,667 |
| Available-for-sale financial assets | (24,000) | 26,667 |
| Cash flow hedges | (667) | (4,000) |
| Gains on property revaluation | 933 | 3,367 |
| Actuarial gains (losses) on defined benefit pension plans | (667) | 1,333 |
| Share of other comprehensive income of associates | 400 | (700) |
| Income tax relating to components of other comprehensive income | 4,667 | (9,334) |
| **Other comprehensive income for the year, net of tax** | (14,000) | 28,000 |
| **TOTAL COMPREHENSIVE INCOME FOR THE YEAR** | 107,250 | 93,500 |
| Total comprehensive income attributable to: | | |
| Owners of the parent | 85,800 | 74,800 |
| Non-controlling interests | 21,450 | 18,700 |
|  | 107,250 | 93,500 |

# 5 The statement of changes in equity

The title of this statement perfectly describes its function. Essentially the statement provides a link between the opening and closing financial position by reconciling movements in net assets (or equity). These movements basically occur due to three types of event:

- gains or losses in the period that are reported in the statement of comprehensive income

- changes due to transactions with the providers of equity. These transactions could be additional investment by the equity providers or a dividend payment to them

- restatements of opening equity that are necessary when changing accounting policies or having discovered a material prior-period error when preparing the current period financial statements.

The example of this statement that is given in IAS 1 appears below.

| | Share capital | Retained earnings | Translation of foreign operations | Available-for-sale financial assets | Cash flow hedges | Revaluation surplus | Total | Non-controlling interests | Total equity |
|---|---|---|---|---|---|---|---|---|---|
| Balance at 1 January 20X6 | 600,000 | 118,100 | (4,000) | 1,600 | 2,000 | - | 717,700 | 29,800 | 747,500 |
| Changes in accounting policy | - | 400 | - | - | - | - | 400 | 100 | 500 |
| Restated balance | 600,000 | 118,500 | (4,000) | 1,600 | 2,000 | - | 718,100 | 29,900 | 748,000 |
| Changes in equity for 20X6 | | | | | | | | | |
| Dividends | - | (10,000) | | | | | 10,000 | | 10,000 |
| Total comprehensive income for the year | - | 53,200 | 6,400 | 16,000 | (2,400) | 1,600 | 74,800 | 18,700 | 93,500 |
| Balance at 31 December 20X6 | 600,000 | 161,700 | 2,400 | 17,600 | (400) | 1,600 | 782,900 | 48,600 | 831,500 |
| Changes in equity for 20X7 | | | | | | | | | |
| Issue of share capital | 50,000 | - | - | - | - | - | 50,000 | - | 50,000 |
| Dividends | - | (15,000) | - | - | - | - | (15,000) | - | (15,000) |
| Total comprehensive income for the year | - | 96,600 | 3,200 | (14,400) | (400) | 800 | 85,800 | 21,450 | 107,250 |
| Transfer to retained earnings | - | 200 | - | - | - | (200) | - | - | - |
| Balance at 31 December 20X7 | 650,000 | 243,500 | 5,600 | 3,200 | (800) | 2,200 | 903,700 | 70,050 | 973,750 |

It is important to notice the links between this statement and the statements in sections 3 and 4. For example, as shown above the total equity at 31 December 20X7 is 973,750, of which 903,700 is attributable to the owners of the parent and 70,050 to the non-controlling interests. The reader should check these figures across to the statement of financial position in section 3. Also it is possible to agree the 31 December 20X7 numbers for share capital and retained earnings from the above statement to the statement of financial position in section3. The 'other components of equity' number that appears in the statement of financial position at 31 December 20X7 is 10,200. From the above statement this is 5,600 (foreign operations) + 3,200 (financial assets) – 800 (cash flow hedges) + 2,200 (revaluation surplus) = 10,200.

Similarly the total comprehensive income for 20X7 per the above statement is 107,250, of which 21,450 is attributable to the non-controlling interest. The reader should check these figures across to the statement of comprehensive income in sections 3 and 4.

## 6  The statement of cash flows

This statement is required by IAS 7 rather than IAS 1 and will be of assistance from a financial analysis viewpoint when considering liquidity issues. An appendix to IAS 7 has pro-forma examples for the statement of cash flows and the most common is given below.

## Cash flows from operating activities

| | | |
|---|---:|---:|
| Profit before taxation | 3,350 | |
| Adjustments for: | | |
| Depreciation | 450 | |
| Foreign exchange loss | 40 | |
| Investment income | (500) | |
| Interest expense | 400 | |
| | 3,740 | |
| Increase in trade and other receivables | (500) | |
| Decrease in inventories | 1,050 | |
| Decrease in trade payables | (1,740) | |
| Cash generated from operations | 2,550 | |
| Interest paid[1] | (270) | |
| Income taxes paid | (900) | |
| *Net cash from operating activities* | | 1,380 |
| **Cash flows from investing activities** | | |
| Acquisition of subsidiary net of cash acquired | (550) | |
| Purchase of property, plant and equipment | (350) | |
| Proceeds from sale of equipment | 20 | |
| Interest received[2] | 200 | |
| Dividends received[2] | 200 | |
| *Net cash used in investing activities* | | (480) |
| **Cash flows from financing activities** | | |
| Proceeds from the issue of share capital | 250 | |
| Proceeds from long-term borrowings | 250 | |
| Payment of finance lease liabilities | (90) | |
| Dividends paid[3] | (1,200) | |
| *Net cash used in financing activities* | | (790) |
| **Net increase in cash and cash equivalents** | | 110 |
| **Cash and cash equivalents at beginning of period** | | 120 |
| **Cash and cash equivalents at end of period** | | 230 |

<sup>1</sup> Interest paid can alternatively be classified as a financing outflow as long as the classification is consistent from period to period.

<sup>2</sup> Interest and dividends received can alternatively be classified as operating inflows as long as the classifications are consistent from period to period.

<sup>3</sup> Dividends paid can alternatively be classified as an operating outflow as long as the classification is consistent from period to period.

The majority of cash flows for a typical entity are reported in the operating section of the statement. Indeed IAS 7 effectively defines an operating cash flow as any cash flow that is not investing or financing. In the above statement there is a difference in the way the operating cash flows are reported compared with the investing or financing cash flows. The investing and financing cash flows are reported directly by identifying the exact source of the inflow or outflow of cash. The operating cash flows are reported indirectly by starting with the profit or loss for the period and making adjustments for items not involving an operating cash flow. Entities are permitted to use this 'indirect' approach for the operating cash flows and many entities do this. However entities are encouraged (although not required) to report operating cash flows using the direct method. Were this to have been done in the statement included above then the operating section of the statement would have been reported as follows:

### Cash flows from operating activities

| | | |
|---|---:|---:|
| Cash receipts from customers | 30,150 | |
| Cash paid to suppliers and employees | (27,600) | |
| Cash generated from operations | 2,550 | |
| Interest paid | (270) | |
| Income taxes paid | (900) | |
| Net cash from operating activities | | 1,380 |

# Chapter summary

The primary financial statements provide the user with information on the financial position, financial performance, and changes in financial position of an entity. In order to successfully analyse these statements you need to be quite clear about the function of each statement.

- The statement of financial position (or balance sheet) provides users with information about the financial position of an entity at a given date.

- The statement of comprehensive income (whether presented as one or two statements) provides the user with information about the financial performance of an entity for a period.

- The statement of changes in equity provides users with information about the change in overall financial position over a period.

- The statement of cash flows (as the name suggests) provides users with information about cash flows over a period.

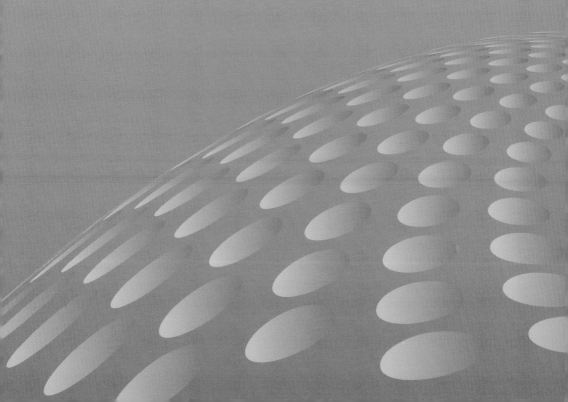

# Chapter 3

## Profitability analysis

## 1 Objectives of the chapter

Having read this chapter you should be able to:

■ calculate the financial ratios that can be used to assess the profitability of an entity

■ describe the links between the ratios

■ discuss reasons for variation in the ratios from period to period, or from entity to entity, distinguishing between those caused by underlying business factors and those caused by accounting policy changes.

## 2 Introduction and financial statements used for analysis

### 2.1 Introduction

In this chapter we will consider how we evaluate the profitability of a business using ratio analysis. Before we look at any specific ratios it is worth making two key general observations.

■ As stated in chapter 1, ratio analysis is of no benefit unless there is a comparative ratio that can be used as a yardstick.

■ Comments such as, 'the ratio has risen or fallen compared with last year' add nothing to the calculation of the ratio – it is necessary to give a logical reason why a ratio has changed to enable the technique to be fully effective. The reasons for the change in a ratio could be due to changed accounting practices (for example, the revaluation of an asset) or to underlying business reasons.

We will use the financial statements that appear below to illustrate the computation of profitability ratios. The data is drawn from a past examination question from the Institute of Chartered Accountants in England and Wales (ICAEW) Financial Reporting paper. The actual question is question 1 from the December 2009 paper.

## 2.2 Financial statements included in ICAEW Financial Reporting Question 1 December 2009

Greenway plc (Greenway) is a listed company operating in the engineering sector. Its recent financial performance has been poor as a result of the global economic downturn. In early 2008 Greenway's management commenced a major restructuring of the business with a focus on improving earnings per share (EPS).

You are a financial analyst at Havenwood plc (Havenwood), an investment company. Havenwood owns approximately 2% of the issued share capital of Greenway. Your manager has given you the following instruction:

"I'd like you to analyse Greenway's financial performance and financial position (including liquidity and solvency) following the restructuring. We'll use your findings as part of the annual review of our investment position."

She has sent you the following information.

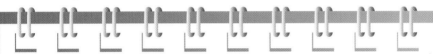

**Extract from operating and financial review for the year ended 30 September 2009**

The management of Greenway has continued to restructure the business during the year including:

■ the sale and operating leaseback of our administrative offices which has generated cash proceeds of £3 million and improved our financial position

■ completing the operational restructuring, that commenced in early 2008, of our administrative processes resulting in staffing and other cost savings that will flow through in 2010

■ product restructuring and the introduction of complementary products into several new business sectors. This has contributed £1.2 million to revenue at gross margins of around 20%

■ the closure of our grinding department. Surplus assets are now for sale. The supply to us of the products previously made in that department is now outsourced. There were quality issues initially with our new outsourcing arrangements which resulted in the temporary loss of some valued customers but we are resolving these issues

■ the renegotiation of contract terms with raw material suppliers. In many cases our credit period has been shortened in return for price reductions.

These factors have contributed to an increase in our EPS with which we measure the success of our management team. The directors propose a final dividend for the year of 10p per share, an increase of 3% from last year.

**Greenway plc – income statement for the year ended 30 September**

|  | Year ended 30 Sept 2009 £'000 | Year ended 30 Sept 2008 £'000 |
|---|---|---|
| Revenue | 14,310 | 14,500 |
| Cost of sales | (11,210) | (11,200) |
| Gross profit | 3,100 | 3,300 |
| Operating expenses | (1,350) | (1,100) |
| Non-recurring items (see note 1) | (100) | (400) |
| Profit from operations | 1,650 | 1,800 |
| Finance costs | (110) | (240) |
| Profit before taxation | 1,540 | 1,560 |
| Income tax | (330) | (470) |
| Profit for the period | 1,210 | 1,090 |
| **EPS** | **60.5p** | **54.9p** |

Greenway plc - statement of financial position at 30 September

| | At 30 Sept 2009 | | At 30 Sept 2008 | |
|---|---|---|---|---|
| | £'000 | £'000 | £'000 | £'000 |
| **ASSETS** | | | | |
| **Non-current assets** | | | | |
| Property, plant & equipment | | 3,620 | | 6,000 |
| **Current assets** | | | | |
| Inventories | 2,410 | | 2,000 | |
| Trade and other receivables | 2,020 | | 1,700 | |
| Cash and cash equivalents | 200 | | 30 | |
| | | 4,630 | | 3,730 |
| **Total assets** | | 8,250 | | 9,730 |
| **EQUITY & LIABILITIES** | | | | |
| **Equity** | | | | |
| Issued capital - £1 ordinary shares | | 2,010 | | 1,990 |
| Retained earnings | | 1,170 | | 150 |
| | | 3,180 | | 2,140 |
| **Non-current liabilities** | | | | |
| Borrowings | | 3,300 | | 5,500 |
| **Current liabilities** | | | | |
| Trade payables | 1,610 | | 1,890 | |
| Other payables | 160 | | 200 | |
| | | 1,770 | | 2,090 |
| **Total equity and liabilities** | | 8,250 | | 9,730 |

## Note 1 Non-recurring items

| | 2009 £'000 | 2008 £'000 |
|---|---|---|
| Gain on sale and leaseback of administrative offices | 500 | - |
| Other restructuring expenses | (600) | (400) |
| | (100) | (400) |

## Additional Information

| | 2009 £'000 | 2008 £'000 |
|---|---|---|
| Cash flow from operations | 420 | 1,950 |
| Research expenditure (included in operating expenses) | 100 | 200 |

# 3 Calculation and explanation of profitability ratios

## 3.1 Return on capital employed (ROCE)

ROCE effectively computes the return (profit) on the funds (capital) invested in the company. When computing ROCE we generally regard 'capital' as equity plus borrowings. We then express the profit before finance costs as a percentage of the capital. For Greenway (see 2.2 above) we have the following:

|  | 2009<br>£'000 | 2008<br>£'000 |
|---|---|---|
| Profit before finance costs (operating profit) | 1,650 | 1,800 |
| Equity | 3,180 | 2,140 |
| Borrowings | 3,300 | 5,500 |
|  | 6,480 | 7,640 |
| So ROCE | 1,650/6,480 = 25.5% | 1,800/7,640 = 23.6% |

There are a number of alternative methods that could be used to compute ROCE, particularly as regards what should be included in 'borrowings'. Examples of items that could be incorporated so as to produce a different figure for 'borrowings' include:

■ deducting cash and cash equivalents from borrowings so as to produce a 'net borrowings' figure

■ adding some or all of the current liabilities to the 'borrowings' figure. Although current liabilities generally get settled relatively quickly, they are often replaced almost instantaneously by newer, equivalent, amounts so that overall they effectively represent a semi-permanent source of finance.

It is not really possible or necessary to identify a single method of computing ROCE. The main factors to bear in mind are to ensure that:

■ both the current year and the prior year ratios (assuming prior year is the basis of comparison) are calculated using exactly the same format

- the 'profit' figure that is used is consistent with the 'capital' figure that is used. This means that whatever borrowings are included in the calculation, the profit figure that is used should be the profit before deducting the finance costs relating to those borrowings.

In this case ROCE has improved since last year. On the face of it, this is a positive sign. However in order to gain further credit in an examination situation, we would need to analyse why this change has occurred rather more deeply. Once again, ratio analysis can help us with this task. This is because the ROCE ratio can effectively be broken down into two 'sub-ratios' due to the following relationship:

$$\frac{\text{Profit}}{\text{Capital}} \text{ could be written as } \frac{\text{Profit}}{\text{Revenue}} \times \frac{\text{Revenue}}{\text{Capital}}$$

This shows that overall profitability is dependent on generating revenue (Revenue/Capital) in such a way that each £1 of revenue earned produces a satisfactory level of profit (Profit/Revenue). We can use these two ratios to give us more insight into why (in this case) ROCE has risen.

## 3.2 Profit/Revenue (Profit margin)

There are a number of ways of calculating profit margin. The method that provides the best link with the ROCE calculation is to use the 'profit' number used in ROCE. If we do that for Greenway then we get:

|  | 2009 £'000 | 2008 £'000 |
|---|---|---|
| Operating profit | 1,650 | 1,800 |
| Revenue | 14,310 | 14,500 |
| So profit margin is | 11.5% | 12.4% |

So the ROCE has not risen because the profit margin has risen – in fact the profit margin has fallen. The reasons for this fall can be analysed further by considering whether it is caused by variations in the gross profit or in other operating expenses. Therefore it is also useful to calculate the gross profit margin. As its name suggests this is the percentage of gross profit to revenue and is computed as follows:

| | 2009 £'000 | 2008 £'000 |
|---|---|---|
| Gross profit | 3,100 | 3,300 |
| Revenue | 14,310 | 14,500 |
| So profit margin is | 21.7% | 22.8% |

So the fall in the overall profit margin is reflected by a fall in the gross margin. This means that Greenway is not generating as much gross profit per £1 of revenue in 2009 as in 2008. It is at this point that sensible suggestions as to why this might have occurred would gain additional marks. In some cases there may well be information included in the examination question that will assist in making these suggestions.

For example, for Greenway, we know from the question that:

■ there has been a change in the sales mix. £1.2 million of the total revenue of £14.31m revenue in 2009 (around 8.4% in total) has been at a gross margin of 20%, less than the overall level for 2009 or 2008. Therefore Greenway has been selling less profitable products in 2009 and this is bound to have an adverse impact on the gross margin

■ the overall level of revenue has fallen since last year. This may or may not be due to problems with the outsourcing of part of the production process. The question does say that some customers were lost as a result of this change. If sales volumes fall, then fixed production costs are allocated to a smaller number of items and the cost per item increases, thus reducing overall profitability

■ there may be one-off costs associated with the outsourcing process that are affecting the gross profit number in 2009. It is at least theoretically possible that some of the assets that are identified as 'for sale' have had to be written down to net selling price where this is lower than existing carrying value

■ there has been a re-negotiation of contract terms leading to price reductions for raw materials. This ought to have resulted in an improvement in the gross margin, rather than the reverse, but it is a relevant factor nevertheless.

In this particular examination question, there is a reasonable amount of information that can be used to explain the change in the gross margin. Where such information is not provided it is acceptable to make reasonable speculation about why changes might have occurred. For example, in the case of Greenway, we do not know:

■ by how much Greenway were able to increase its sales prices in 2009 compared with 2008. Other things being equal, there is a fairly direct relationship between ability to raise prices and the gross profit margin

■ how production costs other than raw material costs (which in this case have apparently been reduced) have changed since 2008. For instance, we have no information regarding the overall change in labour costs since 2008. If we were to state that factors such as these **could** be the reason for the variation in the margin then this should gain marks in an examination.

As well as computing the gross profit margin as a means of explaining the change in the overall profit margin it is also useful to consider the relationship between other operating costs and revenue. For Greenway, we can do this as follows:

| | 2009 £'000 | 2008 £'000 |
|---|---|---|
| Operating expenses | 1,350 | 1,100 |
| Non-recurring items | 100 | 400 |
| | 1,450 | 1,500 |
| Revenue | 14,310 | 14,500 |
| So other operating expenses as a percentage of revenue are | 10.1% | 10.3% |

On the face of it, this shows an improvement, being a lower cost percentage than in 2008. However this ignores that fact that the overall cost number is influenced by non-recurring items. If we computed ongoing operating expenses (1,350) as a percentage of revenue (14,310) for 2009 we would have 9.4%. The equivalent percentage for 2008 is 7.6% (1,100/14,500). Therefore there may be an issue regarding cost control.

## 3.3 Revenue/capital (asset turnover or turnover of capital)

The ratio of revenue to capital measures the extent to which an entity has used the capital provided by investors to generate revenue. It is often referred to as the 'asset turnover ratio' because of the relationship between 'capital' and net assets – the capital of a business is essentially invested in non-current assets and net current assets (often referred to as working capital). The asset turnover is usually expressed as a number, rather than as a percentage.

**In the case of Greenway, the asset turnover ratios are:**

|  | 2009 £'000 | 2008 £'000 |
|---|---|---|
| Revenue | 14,310 | 14,500 |
| Capital | 6,480 | 7,640 |
| So asset turnover ratio equals | 2.2 times | 1.9 times |

On the face of it, this seems a positive trend – we are generating more revenue per £ of capital invested in 2009 than in 2008 and this certainly explains the rise in ROCE we noticed earlier. As with the profit margin ratio, it is possible to investigate this issue in slightly more depth by computing two ratios that can be said to be derived from the asset turnover ratio:

The **non-current asset turnover ratio** is the ratio of revenue to non-current assets and it is computed as shown below:

|  | 2009 £'000 | 2008 £'000 |
|---|---|---|
| Revenue | 14,310 | 14,500 |
| Non-current assets | 3,620 | 6,000 |
| So asset turnover ratio equals | 4.0 times | 2.4 times |

This seems to represent a significant improvement – our investment in non-current assets is significantly reduced since 2008 with minimal impact on revenue so our non-current asset turnover ratio is bound to improve. We need to be careful here, though, because the company has entered into a fairly significant one-off transaction that will have significantly impacted on this ratio. The notes to the question tell us that they sold and leased back their factory under an operating lease. This means that the factory will no longer be included in non-current assets. The proceeds of sale were £3 million and the profit on sale £500,000. This means that the carrying value of the factory at the date of de-recognition was £2.5 million. Therefore the whole of the reduction in non-current assets (and hence the improvement in this ratio) can be explained by this single transaction. If we think about the short and medium term impact of a sale and leaseback on the operating capability of a business we should conclude that it is fairly minimal. Therefore a one-off accounting transaction has been responsible for the change in this ratio, rather than an underlying change in operational efficiency.

Other factors to bear in mind regarding this ratio are that:

- as non-current assets get older and are depreciated more their carrying value will reduce and the ratio will apparently improve in the short term. We must beware when making conclusions on this 'improvement' though as using older assets in our business might not be the best policy in the longer term

- if we replace older assets with new ones (probably a sound long-term strategy) then in the short term this ratio is likely to worsen (to an extent the reverse of the previous factor). Again, we should avoid making a hasty conclusion on changes in this ratio if we are aware that a major asset replacement programme has been carried out

- if we carry out a revaluation of our non-current assets this will increase their carrying value but there is no reason why the revenue of the business should change at all in response to a revaluation. Therefore the non-current asset turnover ratio will be adversely affected but this is the impact of an accounting policy decision rather than an operational impact. At this point it is worth mentioning that a revaluation of non-current assets could also impact on profit margins due to increased depreciation charges

- the ratio is one of a number that measure a relationship between a **period** number (revenue if for an accounting period) and a **point of time** number (assets are as at a particular date). Suppose there is a significant change in assets (up or down) towards the end of the accounting period that might ultimately be expected to impact on revenue and profit. It is doubtful whether the impact will be fully revealed in ratios that are calculated using the revenue or profit for the whole of the existing period and relating revenue or profit to a year end number from the statement of financial position.

The **working capital ratio** is the ratio of revenue to net current assets (or working capital) and is computed as follows:

| | 2009 £'000 | 2008 £'000 |
|---|---|---|
| Revenue | 14,310 | 14,500 |
| Current assets | 4,630 | 3,730 |
| Current liabilities | (1,770) | (2,090) |
| Net current assets | 2,860 | 1,640 |
| So net current asset turnover ratio equals | 5.0 times | 8.8 times |

So the net current asset turnover has reduced substantially since 2008. We will investigate reasons for this reduction in more detail in chapter 5 of this book.

# 4 Overall conclusion regarding the profitability of Greenway

The primary measure of profitability, ROCE, has improved since 2008. This improvement is due entirely to an improvement in the asset turnover ratio. Indeed, profit margins (gross and net) have declined since 2008. The decline in margins is apparently caused by:

■ a change in the sales mix, whereby a new range of less profitable products has been introduced into the portfolio

■ an overall reduction in revenue, partly due to quality issues arising when a key production procedure was outsourced

■ an overall rise in other operating expenses (partly offset by a reduction in 'unusual losses').

The improvement in the asset turnover ratio is caused by an improvement in the non-current asset turnover ratio. This in turn is caused by a one-off accounting transaction (the sale and leaseback of a factory) rather than an underlying operational improvement. In the longer term this will pose further challenges for Greenway when the lease comes to an end and needs to be renegotiated or the factory vacated.

The net current asset turnover ratio (or working capital ratio) has declined significantly since last year. We will investigate the constituent parts of this decline in chapter 5.

Hopefully through the processes we have introduced in this chapter you can begin to see how we dissect the financial information provided, plus any accompanying supporting notes, to make reasoned conclusions on profitability.

# 5 Profitability analysis – shareholder perspective

In this chapter we have based our analysis of profitability on ROCE, the ratio of profit to capital. The 'capital' figure we have used is equity capital plus borrowings. This is usually of most benefit in analysing overall corporate profitability as entities are financed partly by equity and partly by borrowings.

If we are analysing profitability purely from the perspective of the providers of equity capital then it is often useful to calculate (probably in addition to ROCE) profitability in a more 'shareholder specific' way. The ratio we compute is the **Return on Shareholders Funds** (ROSF). ROSF is calculated as follows:

$$\frac{\text{Profit attributable to the equity shareholders}}{\text{Equity}} \quad \text{(usually the profit after tax)}$$

In the case of Greenway, ROSF would be:

|  | 2009 £'000 | 2008 £'000 |
|---|---|---|
| Profit after tax | 1,210 | 1,090 |
| Equity | 3,180 | 2,140 |
| So ROSF equals | 38.1% | 50.9% |

So the trend in ROSF is very different from the trend in ROCE. ROCE tends to be the more reliable measure of overall profitability so it would not usually be appropriate to compute ROSF without ROCE. Nevertheless it is necessary to explain why ROCE has moved one way and ROSF another.

■ The key factor driving the improvement in ROCE is the sale and leaseback of the factory. The profit on sale and subsequent interest saving has boosted profits attributable to the equity shareholders. However an even more significant change to the financial statements as a result of this transaction is that a substantial part of the sales proceeds were used to reduce borrowings. This reduction in **overall** capital employed has **not** been reflected in a reduction in equity capital. Therefore the consequential improvement in ROCE has not been seen in ROSF. As we have already seen, other drivers of profitability, profit margin and net current asset turnover, have shown a declining trend.

- A significant component of the increase in equity has been due to the profit for the current period. Because of previous losses the retained earnings at the start of the period were only £150,000. The current year profit of £1,210,000 has caused these to rise to £1,170,000 (there must have been a dividend payment of £190,000 during 2009). As a result of this phenomenon an increase of around 11% in profit after tax has led to an increase of around 49% in equity (the change in share capital is relatively insignificant).

The placement of the material regarding ROSF at the end of the chapter is deliberate. If you are going to use it as an interpretation tool, it is recommended that you first carry out a full ROCE analysis and then proceed to considering ROSF.

We will look at other aspects of the analysis of the financial statements of Greenway in the chapters that follow.

## Chapter summary

The primary ratio that measures the profitability of an entity is the ROCE. ROCE is the profit made by an entity expressed as a percentage of the capital invested, both equity capital and borrowings. For analysis purposes, the ratio can be usefully divided into:

- profit margin (operating profit/revenue)

- asset turnover (revenue/capital).

Where variations in the ratio occur it is important to ascertain whether these are caused by business issues (such as selling a greater proportion of products that have a higher or lower profit margin than the average) or accounting issues (such as a decision to revalue assets).

When analysing profitability purely from the perspective of the equity shareholders it may be useful to compute ROSF in addition to ROCE. ROSF is the profit attributable to the equity shareholders expressed as a percentage of equity as shown in the statement of financial position.

# Chapter 4

## Liquidity and gearing

## 1   Objectives of the chapter

Having read this chapter you should be able to:

■ compute the two key liquidity ratios from figures in the statement of financial position and discuss which of them provides the more appropriate measure of liquidity

■ explain why liquidity ratios may vary significantly depending on the type of entity

■ discuss the meaning of 'gearing' and compute gearing ratios

■ explain the link between liquidity and gearing

■ explain how the statement of cash flows can be used to assess the liquidity of an entity.

## 2   Computation of liquidity ratios from the statement of financial position

### 2.1   The underlying financial information to be used in this chapter

**Extract from operating and financial review for the year ended 30 September 2009**

The management of Greenway has continued to restructure the business during the year including:

■ the sale and operating leaseback of our administrative offices which has generated cash proceeds of £3 million and improved our financial position

■ completing the operational restructuring, that commenced in early 2008, of our administrative processes resulting in staffing and other cost savings that will flow through in 2010

- product restructuring and the introduction of complementary products into several new business sectors. This has contributed £1.2 million to revenue at gross margins of around 20%

- the closure of our grinding department. Surplus assets are now for sale. The supply to us of the products previously made in that department is now outsourced. There were quality issues initially with our new outsourcing arrangements which resulted in the temporary loss of some valued customers but we are resolving these issues

- the renegotiation of contract terms with raw material suppliers. In many cases our credit period has been shortened in return for price reductions.

These factors have contributed to an increase in our EPS with which we measure the success of our management team. The directors propose a final dividend for the year of 10p per share, an increase of 3% from last year.

**Greenway plc – income statement for the year ended 30 September**

|  | Year ended 30 Sept 2009 | Year ended 30 Sept 2008 |
|---|---|---|
|  | £'000 | £'000 |
| Revenue | 14,310 | 14,500 |
| Cost of sales | (11,210) | (11,200) |
| Gross profit | 3,100 | 3,300 |
| Operating expenses | (1,350) | (1,100) |
| Non-recurring items (see note 1) | (100) | (400) |
| Profit from operations | 1,650 | 1,800 |
| Finance costs | (110) | (240) |
| Profit before taxation | 1,540 | 1,560 |
| Income tax | (330) | (470) |
| Profit for the period | 1,210 | 1,090 |
| EPS | 60.5p | 54.9p |

# Greenway plc - statement of financial position at 30 September

|  | At 30 Sept 2009 | | At 30 Sept 2008 | |
|---|---|---|---|---|
|  | £'000 | £'000 | £'000 | £'000 |
| **ASSETS** | | | | |
| **Non-current assets** | | | | |
| Property, plant & equipment | | 3,620 | | 6,000 |
| **Current assets** | | | | |
| Inventories | 2,410 | | 2,000 | |
| Trade and other receivables | 2,020 | | 1,700 | |
| Cash and cash equivalents | 200 | | 30 | |
|  | | 4,630 | | 3,730 |
| **Total assets** | | 8,250 | | 9,730 |
| **EQUITY & LIABILITIES** | | | | |
| **Equity** | | | | |
| Issued capital - £1 ordinary shares | | 2,010 | | 1,990 |
| Retained earnings | | 1,170 | | 150 |
|  | | 3,180 | | 2,140 |
| **Non-current liabilities** | | | | |
| Borrowings | | 3,300 | | 5,500 |
| **Current liabilities** | | | | |
| Trade payables | 1,610 | | 1,890 | |
| Other payables | 160 | | 200 | |
|  | | 1,770 | | 2,090 |
| **Total equity and liabilities** | | 8,250 | | 9,730 |

# Note 1 Non-recurring items

|  | 2009 £'000 | 2008 £'000 |
|---|---|---|
| Gain on sale and leaseback of administrative offices | 500 | - |
| Other restructuring expenses | (600) | (400) |
|  | (100) | (400) |

## Additional Information

|  | 2009 £'000 | 2008 £'000 |
|---|---|---|
| Cash flow from operations | 420 | 1,950 |
| Research expenditure (included in operating expenses) | 100 | 200 |

## 2.2 Computation and explanation of the current ratio

The current ratio is one of the most straightforward ratios to compute. It is simply the ratio of current assets to current liabilities. For Greenway the ratio is as follows:

|  | 2009 £'000 | 2008 £'000 |
|---|---|---|
| Current assets | 4,630 | 3,730 |
| Current liabilities | 1,770 | 2,090 |
| So current ratio equals | 2.6 | 1.8 |

The current ratio is a valid measure of liquidity as it compares current assets, which should in theory be capable of being turned into cash fairly quickly, with the current liabilities, which effectively need to be settled in cash relatively quickly. For most entities, you would expect the current ratio to be well in excess of 1 as this means the entity ought to be able to settle its existing short term obligations out of its existing current assets.

You can see that as far as Greenway is concerned the current ratio is well in excess of 1 for both years and indeed it has risen considerably from 2008 to 2009. On the face of it this might lead us to conclude that the liquidity of Greenway was better at the end of 2009 than at the end of 2008. We need to be careful however before making too definite a conclusion regarding liquidity before examining other evidence. There are a number of issues to remember:

- one reason why the current ratio has risen so much is the revision of payment terms to suppliers. This has reduced current liabilities and therefore increased the current ratio. Suppliers are now giving us less credit so this means we need to find cash more quickly. This could in fact put pressure on our cash balances

- the other reason(s) for the rise in the ratio is the rise in both inventories and trade receivables. We would need to investigate why these rises have occurred. If the rise in inventories and trade receivables is caused by expansion of the business then this would be considered to be perfectly acceptable provided it was in line with the amount of expansion that had occurred. However if we examine the income statement of Greenway we see that in fact no expansion has occurred. Indeed, revenue has actually fallen in 2009 compared with 2008. Therefore the rise in inventory could indicate potentially obsolete inventory and the rise in trade receivables a difficulty in collecting cash from customers. Neither of these two rises would be regarded as good news from a liquidity viewpoint.

The computation of the quick ratio (sometimes referred to as the acid test ratio) is quite similar to that of the current ratio. It is the ratio of current assets minus inventories to current liabilities. The argument for using this ratio as an alternative measure of liquidity to the current ratio is that in many entities the inventories cannot be turned into cash sufficiently quickly to settle the current liabilities.

For Greenway the quick ratio is as follows:

|  | 2009 £'000 | 2008 £'000 |
|---|---|---|
| Current assets less inventories | 2,220 | 1,730 |
| Current liabilities | 1,770 | 2,090 |
| So quick ratio equals | 1.3 | 0.8 |

If we were using the quick ratio as a measure of liquidity we would normally expect it to be in excess of 1 for the same reasons as those given for the current ratio above. Just like the current ratio the quick ratio seems to have improved significantly compared to last year. In fact the quick ratio for 2008 (0.8) would often be regarded as unsatisfactorily low and the ratio for 2009 much more acceptable. However as with the current ratio we need to interpret changes in the ratio with caution. The majority of current assets excluding inventories is (for 2008 and 2009) trade receivables. The key reason for the increase in the ratio is the 19% increase in trade receivables from 2008 to 2009. In the same period revenue actually went down slightly so Greenway might be experiencing problems collecting cash from its customers.  In summary, we need to be quite careful when making conclusions about liquidity from either of the two ratios we have computed so far in this chapter without considering other information.

## 3 Explanation of reasons for variation in liquidity ratios from entity to entity

### 3.1 Opening remarks

In this section we will seek to answer two questions.

■ Which of the two liquidity ratios we have computed so far is the better measure of liquidity?

■ What is a 'satisfactory' measure of the liquidity ratio?

### 3.2 Current ratio versus quick ratio; which is the better measure of liquidity?

The difference between the current ratio and the quick ratio is that the current ratio includes inventories in the top half of the ratio and the quick ratio does not. Therefore when computing the current ratio we are inferring that inventories can be turned into cash sufficiently quickly to settle the current liabilities of the entity. When computing the quick ratio we are inferring the opposite.

Which of the two inferences is the more appropriate depends crucially on the nature of the inventory. The decision will vary from entity to entity. For an entity in the retail sector, where the time taken to turn inventory into cash is typically fairly short, then the current ratio is likely to be the more appropriate. In the construction sector the quick ratio is likely to be more relevant. To summarise, the shorter the working capital cycle – the time between paying for raw materials to receiving cash for finished products – the more likely it is that the current ratio is the better liquidity ratio to work with.

### 3.3 What is a satisfactory measure of the liquidity ratio?

We have already stated that, in general, entities would expect their liquidity ratio (however computed) to be in excess of 1. However this statement is a generalisation. Many entities in the retail sector are able to operate with liquidity ratios far less than 1 without any liquidity problems whatsoever. The reason for this is because of the length of their working capital cycle.

For some retail entities, the working capital cycle is negative – meaning that some entities receive payment for the sale of their products before they have paid their suppliers for them. This is possible because such entities will purchase products on normal credit terms of 30 days or longer, immediately offer them for sale, then sell them very quickly due to their nature (e.g. dairy products or non-frozen meat) on a cash basis.

This means that such entities can rely on cash from the sale of goods they have not yet purchased to settle existing current liabilities. As a result, such entities can operate quite comfortably and consistently on liquidity ratios of a lot less than 1.

If a construction entity had a liquidity ratio of less than 1 this would be very concerning because, unless the entity were able to raise cash from alternative sources, it would be likely to find itself unable to settle its current liabilities as they fall due. This teaches us 2 important lessons about interpreting the liquidity ratios.

■ We need to be very cautious about comparing the liquidity ratio of one entity with that of another unless we are sure they operate in a similar sector.

■ When comparing the liquidity ratio of an entity from one period to another it is sudden variations in the ratio compared with a longer term trend that should be our focus.

## 4 Gearing and gearing ratios

### 4.1 The meaning of 'gearing'

The gearing of an entity is a description of the relationship between its equity capital and its borrowings. Although both provide cash for an entity to use there are two very significant differences between equity capital and borrowings.

■ Equity capital is not 'repayable' but borrowings are normally repayable on a fixed date or even, in the case of some short term borrowings, on demand.

■ There is no automatic right for the providers of equity capital to receive a return on their investment. Their return – usually in the form of a dividend payment, is at the discretion of the directors of the entity. On the other hand the providers of borrowed funds normally receive a guaranteed annual return – usually in the form of an interest payment.

## 4.2 The calculation of gearing ratios

There is no single method of computing a gearing ratio. Any ratio that compares the relationship between equity capital and borrowings would be acceptable in theory. Generally gearing ratios are computed in such a way that the greater the proportion of total funding that is provided by borrowings the greater is the gearing ratio. In practice this usually means computing gearing ratios in one of two ways:

The first is the ratio of borrowings to borrowings plus equity. This is always going to be less than 100%. The second is the ratio of borrowings to equity, which could easily be more than 100% in certain cases. For Greenway, we have the following:

|  | 2009 | 2008 |
|---|---|---|
|  | £'000 | £'000 |
| Borrowings | 3,300 | 5,500 |
| Equity | 3,180 | 2,140 |
| Borrowings plus equity | 6,480 | 7,640 |
| First gearing ratio | 51% | 72% |
| Second gearing ratio | 104% | 257% |

When we compute gearing ratios in this manner we see that in both cases the gearing has fallen in 2009 compared with 2008. There are broadly two reasons for this.

- The profit made in 2009 has increased the equity of Greenway.

- The borrowings have been reduced by £2.2 million since 2008, this reduction apparently having been financed by the proceeds of the sale and leaseback of the administrative offices.

So is the reduction in gearing a good thing or not? As stated earlier for the current ratio and the quick ratio we need to interpret these ratios with caution. Gearing measures the relationship between borrowings and equity capital. It is usually beneficial for an entity to be financed at least in part by borrowings because the providers of borrowed funds normally require a lower return on their investment than the providers of equity capital. This is because the providers of borrowed funds are taking much less risk than the providers of equity capital. The providers of borrowed funds are normally guaranteed an annual return and (unless the entity has going concern issues) are guaranteed repayment. Therefore borrowed finance is normally cheaper for the entity than equity finance.

A counter-argument to the above is that a highly geared entity (i.e. one with a high proportion of funds provided by borrowings) causes additional risk for the providers of equity capital. Consider the following example.

| Entity | A | B |
| --- | --- | --- |
| | £'000 | £'000 |
| Borrowings (10% before tax) | 12,000 | 4,000 |
| Equity | 4,000 | 12,000 |
| Total 'capital' | 16,000 | 16,000 |
| | | |
| Operating profit | 3,200 | 3,200 |
| Finance cost | (1,200) | (400) |
| Profit before tax | 2,000 | 2,800 |
| Income tax expense (assume 25%) | (500) | (700) |
| Profit after tax (theoretically available for a dividend) | 1,500 | 2,100 |

Let us consider the impact of both a 50% rise and a 50% fall in operating profit on the profit after tax (available for a dividend to the providers of equity capital).

**50% rise**

| Entity | A | B |
| --- | --- | --- |
| | £'000 | £'000 |
| Operating profit | 4,800 | 4,800 |
| Finance cost | (1,200) | (400) |
| Profit before tax | 3,600 | 4,400 |
| Income tax expense (assume 25%) | (900) | (1,100) |
| Profit after tax (theoretically available for a dividend) | 2,700 | 3,300 |
| **% increase in profit after tax given a 50% rise in operating profit** | 80% | 57% |

**50% fall**

| Entity | A | B |
|---|---|---|
| | £'000 | £'000 |
| Operating profit | 1,600 | 1,600 |
| Finance cost | (1,200) | (400) |
| Profit before tax | 400 | 1,200 |
| Income tax expense (assume 25%) | (100) | (300) |
| Profit after tax (theoretically available for a dividend) | 300 | 900 |
| **% decrease in profit after tax given a 50% fall in operating profit** | 80% | 57% |

For both entities the percentage change in profits after tax (available for dividend) is greater than the percentage change in operating profit. This is because, if we regard the operating profits as a 'cake', the slice of the cake that the providers of borrowed funds receive is the same whatever the size of the cake. This means that the change in the size of the rest of the cake will be of a larger proportion than the change in size of the cake as a whole.

The change is more marked in the case of entity A because the level of gearing in A is higher than in B – notice that the total capital available to the 2 entities is the same. This shows us that the higher the level of gearing the greater is the variation in the profits available for the providers of equity capital for a given variation in operating profit. This in turn means that in a highly geared entity the returns available to the providers of equity capital are subject to more risk than in an entity where the gearing is lower. Therefore, given the economic relationship between risk and return, the providers of equity capital in a highly geared entity will require a higher return on their investment than those in an entity that is less highly geared. This will make raising additional equity capital more difficult in a highly geared entity.

So gearing can be beneficial for the entity – in the form of cheaper finance, but too high a level of gearing can be unacceptable for the providers of equity capital. Theories of gearing can be fairly complex but the majority of theorists would agree that, for most entities, the overall cost of capital falls for a time as gearing rises from relatively low levels. However if gearing continues to rise beyond an 'optimum' level then the overall cost of capital will tend to rise also as the additional return required by the providers of equity capital will outweigh the relatively cheap cost of borrowed funds.

It is difficult to quantify where exactly this optimum level of gearing is for each entity. However in general it is reasonable to suggest that where the gearing ratio is over 50% (first ratio) or 100% (second ratio) it would benefit from being reduced. Therefore, for Greenway, the change in gearing from 2008 to 2009 is likely to be regarded as desirable.

Before we move on, however, we need to add a note of caution regarding the conclusion we have just reached regarding the change in gearing. In the case of Greenway a key reason for the fall in gearing has been the repayment of borrowings out of the proceeds of the sale and leaseback of the administrative offices. The leaseback arrangement has been classified as an operating lease so the offices are removed from the statement of financial position. Had the leaseback arrangement been classified as a finance lease then the offices would have remained in the statement of financial position and the sales proceeds would have been recognised as a borrowing so the sale and leaseback would have initially caused a substantial increase in gearing. Lease classification is a very subjective matter and this fall in gearing is linked, at least in part, to the assessment of the leaseback arrangement as operating. Potential future developments in the area of lease accounting will abolish the distinction between operating leases and finance leases and require lessees to include an asset and associated liability for all material leases. Therefore the fall in gearing could be said to be due to accounting conventions rather than underlying business reasons.

# 5 The link between liquidity and gearing

This relationship is to a large degree based on the discussion we started in section 4. If an entity wishes to raise cash it can essentially do this in two ways:

## 5.1 It can generate the cash from its own operations

Ultimately all entities will need to raise cash in this way as the providers of borrowed funds will require repaying at some stage and the providers of equity capital will only invest more capital in the entity if they are satisfied in the internal cash-generating ability of the entity. We will consider the internal cash generating capacity of an entity in section 6 of this chapter.

## 5.2 It can raise the cash from external investors

When an entity seeks to raise cash from external investors there are, at least in theory, two options:

- borrow the cash

- raise additional cash from the equity investors.

If gearing is high (and as stated in section 4 it is difficult to quantify exactly what 'high' means in this context) then raising cash from external investors can prove difficult. Increasing borrowings will only make gearing higher and could increase the overall cost of capital to unacceptable levels. In particular there will be a greater fixed commitment to pay interest or other forms of finance cost whatever the level of profits.

The alternative is to seek to raise more cash from the providers of equity capital. Where an entity is highly geared equity investors are likely to require a higher return on their investment and so are likely to be prepared to invest less cash in a particular situation than if the gearing is lower. This means that, overall, entities that are highly geared are likely to find it more difficult to raise cash from external providers. This means that, unless their operating cash flow is strong (see section 6 below for more details) highly geared entities are more likely to suffer liquidity problems than those that are not so highly geared.

The issue of the relative vulnerability of a highly geared entity to variations in profits can be given some numerical focus by the interest cover ratio. This measures the ratio of the operating profit (profit before finance cost) to the finance cost for the period. The lower this ratio, the more likely it is that a fall in operating profit will lead to an overall loss.

**For Greenway, the ratio is as follows:**

|  | 2009<br>£'000 | 2008<br>£'000 |
|---|---|---|
| Operating profit | 1650 | 1,800 |
| Finance cost | 110 | 240 |
| So interest cover | 15 | 7.5 |

For Greenway it would appear that the interest cover ratio is perfectly satisfactory for both years. The increase from 2009 to 2008 gives us additional assurance that, at current levels of finance cost, a fall in the operating profit is unlikely to lead to an overall loss for the entity.

## 6 The use of the statement of cash flows to assess liquidity

All the liquidity analysis we have performed so far in this chapter has focused on ratio analysis. Whilst this is often useful it is also beneficial to assess liquidity over a time period by comparing cash generated with cash used. The ideal way of doing this is by reviewing the statement of cash flows. The statement of cash flows for Greenway for 2009 is given below:

| | £'000 | £'000 |
|---|---|---|
| **Cash flows from operating activities** | | |
| Profit before taxation | 1,540 | |
| Adjustments for: | | |
| Depreciation | 280 | |
| Profit on sale of administrative offices | (500) | |
| Finance cost | 110 | |
| | 1,430 | |
| Increase in trade and other receivables | (320) | |
| Increase in inventories | (410) | |
| Decrease in trade payables | (280) | |
| Cash generated from operations | 420 | |
| Interest paid | (110) | |
| Income taxes paid | (370) | |
| *Net cash from operating activities* | | (60) |

**Cash flows from investing activities**

| | | |
|---|---:|---:|
| Purchase of property, plant and equipment | (400) | |
| Proceeds from sale of administrative offices | 3,000 | |
| Net cash raised from investing activities | | 2,600 |
| Cash flows from financing activities | | |
| Proceeds from the issue of share capital | 20 | |
| Payment of long-term borrowings | (2,200) | |
| Dividends paid | (190) | |
| Net cash used in financing activities | | (2,370) |
| Net increase in cash and cash equivalents | | 170 |
| Cash and cash equivalents at beginning of period | | 30 |
| Cash and cash equivalents at end of period | | 200 |

This statement shows a picture of liquidity that is somewhat disturbing. At the root of the problems is the level of cash generated from operating activities – not even enough to cover interest, tax and dividend payments. A key reason for this unsatisfactory state of affairs appears to be the additional investment in working capital of £1,010,000 (£320,000 + £410,000 + £280,000) at the end of 2009 compared with 2008 (we will investigate this issue further in chapter 5).

It appears that Greenway has relied heavily on the sale of its administrative offices to maintain (and even slightly increase) its cash balances. The problem for the future is that this source of cash is a 'one-off' and carries with it future cash commitments in the form of rental payments. It appears that Greenway needs to address the reasons for the significant decline in operating cash flow (information given in the question indicates that it was £1,950,000 in 2008) and seek to restore it to previous levels in 2010 and beyond.

# Chapter summary

- The two key liquidity ratios that can be computed from the statement of financial position are the current ratio (the ratio of current assets to current liabilities) and the quick ratio (the ratio of current assets minus inventories to current liabilities).

- Both the current ratio and the quick ratio compare the assets that are considered to be a reasonably quick source of cash to the liabilities that need to be settled relatively quickly. The difference is the perception of whether inventories can be regarded as a reasonably quick source of future cash.

- Whether the current ratio or the quick ratio is the best measure of liquidity depends on the type of entity. Retail and similar entities are more likely to use the current ratio whilst construction type entities would tend to use the quick ratio.

- For the majority of entities you would expect the liquidity ratio (whichever is the more appropriate) to be more than 1. However entities with a very short working capital cycle can operate satisfactorily with a liquidity ratio that is consistently less than 1.

- The gearing of an entity measures the relationship between its equity capital and its borrowings. Generally the greater the proportion of borrowings to total capital the higher is the gearing.

- Whilst some degree of gearing is desirable for most entities too high a level can make an entity unstable due to the large fixed commitment to pay interest whatever the level of underlying profit.

- A highly geared entity can have problems raising external capital due to the reluctance of investors to invest equity capital (because of the high rate of return required) and the further instability that would be introduced by further borrowings.

- The statement of cash flows is very useful in assessing the liquidity of an entity as it shows the sources of cash and how that cash has been used.

# Chapter 5

## Efficiency analysis and working capital management

## 1 Objectives of the chapter

Having read this chapter you should be able to:

- recall the link between profitability and efficiency of capital

- compute and analyse the overall efficiency ratios for non-current assets and working capital

- compute and analyse the three constituent parts of the overall working capital efficiency ratio

- explain the link between working capital management and liquidity

- understand the link between the efficiency ratios and the other ratios that provide information regarding profitability – 'the ratio pyramid'.

### 1.1 The underlying financial information to be used in this chapter

**Extract from operating and financial review for the year ended 30 September 2009**

The management of Greenway has continued to restructure the business during the year including:

- the sale and operating leaseback of our administrative offices which has generated cash proceeds of £3 million and improved our financial position

- completing the operational restructuring, that commenced in early 2008, of our administrative processes resulting in staffing and other cost savings that will flow through in 2010

- product restructuring and the introduction of complementary products into several new business sectors. This has contributed £1.2 million to revenue at gross margins of around 20%

- the closure of our grinding department. Surplus assets are now for sale. The supply to us of the products previously made in that department is now outsourced. There were quality issues initially with our new outsourcing arrangements which resulted in the temporary loss of some valued customers but we are resolving these issues

- the renegotiation of contract terms with raw material suppliers. In many cases our credit period has been shortened in return for price reductions.

These factors have contributed to an increase in our EPS with which we measure the success of our management team. The directors propose a final dividend for the year of 10p per share, an increase of 3% from last year.

**Greenway plc – income statement for the year ended 30 September**

|  | Year ended 30 Sept 2009 £'000 | Year ended 30 Sept 2008 £'000 |
|---|---|---|
| Revenue | 14,310 | 14,500 |
| Cost of sales | (11,210) | (11,200) |
| Gross profit | 3,100 | 3,300 |
| Operating expenses | (1,350) | (1,100) |
| Non-recurring items (see note 1) | (100) | (400) |
| Profit from operations | 1,650 | 1,800 |
| Finance costs | (110) | (240) |
| Profit before taxation | 1,540 | 1,560 |
| Income tax | (330) | (470) |
| Profit for the period | 1,210 | 1,090 |
| **EPS** | **60.5p** | **54.9p** |

# Greenway plc - statement of financial position at 30 September

| | At 30 Sept 2009 | | At 30 Sept 2008 | |
|---|---|---|---|---|
| | £'000 | £'000 | £'000 | £'000 |
| **ASSETS** | | | | |
| **Non-current assets** | | | | |
| Property, plant & equipment | | 3,620 | | 6,000 |
| **Current assets** | | | | |
| Inventories | 2,410 | | 2,000 | |
| Trade and other receivables | 2,020 | | 1,700 | |
| Cash and cash equivalents | 200 | | 30 | |
| | | 4,630 | | 3,730 |
| **Total assets** | | 8,250 | | 9,730 |
| **EQUITY & LIABILITIES** | | | | |
| **Equity** | | | | |
| Issued capital - £1 ordinary shares | | 2,010 | | 1,990 |
| Retained earnings | | 1,170 | | 150 |
| | | 3,180 | | 2,140 |
| **Non-current liabilities** | | | | |
| Borrowings | | 3,300 | | 5,500 |
| **Current liabilities** | | | | |
| Trade payables | 1,610 | | 1,890 | |
| Other payables | 160 | | 200 | |
| | | 1,770 | | 2,090 |
| Total equity and liabilities | | 8,250 | | 9,730 |

## Note 1 Non-recurring items

|  | 2009 £'000 | 2008 £'000 |
|---|---|---|
| Gain on sale and leaseback of administrative offices | 500 | - |
| Other restructuring expenses | (600) | (400) |
|  | (100) | (400) |

## Additional Information

|  | 2009 £'000 | 2008 £'000 |
|---|---|---|
| Cash flow from operations | 420 | 1,950 |
| Research expenditure (included in operating expenses) | 100 | 200 |

## 2 The link between profitability and efficiency of capital

In chapter 3 we learned that the primary ratio of profitability is Return on Capital Employed (ROCE). ROCE is the ratio of profit from operations to total capital (both equity capital and borrowings). We further stated that ROCE can be broken down into 2 main constituent parts:

■ profit margin (the ratio of operating profit to revenue)

■ asset turnover (the ratio of revenue to total capital).

The sub-division of ROCE reminds us that in order to be profitable an entity needs to be able to:

■ generate revenue that is greater than the costs incurred in generating that revenue (this aspect of profitability is measured by the profit margin), and to

■ generate a sufficient volume of sales to produce a satisfactory level of profit to capital invested (this aspect of profitability is measured by the asset turnover ratio).

We computed ROCE, profit margin and asset turnover.

**ROCE**

|  | 2009 £'000 | 2008 £'000 |
|---|---|---|
| Profit before finance costs (profit from operations) | 1,650 | 1,800 |
| Equity | 3,180 | 2,140 |
| Borrowings | 3,300 | 5,500 |
|  | 6,480 | 7,640 |
| So ROCE | 1,650/6,480 = 25.5% | 1,800/7,640 = 23.6% |

## Profit margin

|  | 2009 £'000 | 2008 £'000 |
|---|---|---|
| Profit from operations | 1,650 | 1,800 |
| Revenue | 14,310 | 14,500 |
| So profit margin is | 11.5% | 12.4% |

## Asset turnover

|  | 2009 £'000 | 2008 £'000 |
|---|---|---|
| Revenue | 14,310 | 14,500 |
| Capital | 6,480 | 7,640 |
| So asset turnover ratio equals | 2.2 times | 1.9 times |

We will focus on the asset turnover in this chapter as it is this ratio that measures the efficiency with which an entity is using its capital.

## 3 The overall efficiency ratios for non-current assets and working capital

We stated in chapter 3 that, because total capital is basically non-current assets plus **net** current assets (commonly referred to as 'working capital'. We can investigate the efficiency ratio in two parts.

### 3.1 Non-current asset turnover ratio

As stated in chapter 3 this is the ratio of revenue to non-current assets.

|  | 2009 | 2008 |
|---|---|---|
|  | £'000 | £'000 |
| Revenue | 14,310 | 14,500 |
| Non-current assets | 3,620 | 6,000 |
| So asset turnover ratio equals | 4.0 times | 2.4 times |

On the face of it is seems as if this ratio has improved significantly and we are using our non-current assets much more efficiently in 2009 than we were in 2008. We discussed the reasons why this conclusion may need to be tempered with caution in chapter 3. These reasons are summarised below.

■ The reason for the fall is almost entirely due to the sale and operating leaseback of the administrative offices. This is a one-off transaction that, had the leaseback resulted in a finance lease, would have produced a much lower non-current asset turnover so there does not appear to be any underlying operational improvement here.

■ The ratio of revenue to non-current assets is one of a number that measure a relationship between a period number (revenue if for an accounting period) and a point of time number ( non-current assets are as at a particular date). If there is a significant change in assets (up or down) towards the end of the accounting period that might ultimately be expected to impact on revenue and profit. It is doubtful whether the impact will be fully revealed in ratios that are calculated using the revenue or profit for the whole of the existing period and relating revenue or profit to a year-end number from the statement of financial position.

## 3.2 Working capital turnover ratio

As stated in chapter 3 this is the ratio of revenue to net current assets (or working capital) and it is computed as follows.

|  | 2009 £'000 | 2008 £'000 |
|---|---|---|
| Revenue | 14,310 | 14,500 |
| Current assets | 4,630 | 3,730 |
| Current liabilities | (1,770) | (2,090) |
| Net current assets | 2,860 | 1,640 |
| So net current asset turnover ratio equals | 5.0 times | 8.8 times |

This ratio has declined significantly and the reason for the decline needs to be investigated further.

## 4 Computation and analysis of the three constituent parts of the overall working capital efficiency ratio

### 4.1 Introduction

The three main components of working capital are inventory, trade receivables and trade payables. When we investigate variations in the overall level of working capital we usually focus on these three components in turn.

### 4.2 Inventory

There are two ways of analysing changes in the level of inventory using ratios. Both methods involve a comparison of the year-end inventory with the cost of inventory sold in the period (cost of sales). In both cases, this gives us an indication of the 'real' level of inventory of the entity.

The first of these ratios is the inventory turnover ratio. This is the ratio of cost of sales to closing inventory. The ratio for Greenway for 2008 and 2009 is as shown below:

|  | 2009 £'000 | 2008 £'000 |
| --- | --- | --- |
| Cost of sales | 11,210 | 11,200 |
| Closing inventory | 2,410 | 2,000 |
| So inventory turnover ratio equals | 4.7 times | 5.6 times |

In most circumstances a decline in this ratio is not a good sign. It normally means that the inventory is taking longer to sell. This could in turn give rise to the risk of obsolete inventory in the future. If we are interpreting audited financial statements we should have reasonable assurance that the inventory is not currently obsolete. If it were, then it should already have been written down or written off under the applicable accounting standard. However if the financial statements are stated to be 'draft' or 'unaudited' it might be necessary to query the carrying value of the inventory in the financial statements.

Before making too definitive a conclusion on changes in the inventory turnover ratio we need to bear the following factors in mind.

■ Inventory turnover is one of the ratios that compare a point of time figure (closing inventory) with a period figure (the cost of sales for a period). A significant change in inventory (up or down) just before the year-end would have very little impact on cost of sales and so this ratio would change significantly in such circumstances. Such changes are not necessarily indicative of normal inventory levels so the conclusion needs to be tempered.

■ If an entity is planning significant expansion in the future then it will need to build up its inventory to meet the increased requirements of its customers. The inventory turnover compares closing inventory with past usage whereas in reality the closing inventory is going to meet future requirements. If expansion of the business is gradual over time then this does not necessarily make the ratio analysis misleading as we are comparing the inventory ratio over time. However an expansion at a rate that is significantly greater than in previous periods could easily make the comparison potentially misleading.

Before we leave this ratio it is worth stating that levels of inventory turnover vary considerably from entity to entity depending on the nature of the business. It would not be appropriate to compare the inventory turnover across different entities unless we were sure they operated in the same, or similar, business sectors.

An alternative method of analysing the 'real' level of inventory is to compute the **inventory days**. This is the ratio of closing inventory to 1 day's cost of sales. It measures the number of days it would take to sell the closing inventory assuming the level of future activity is the same as the average level of activity in the previous period. The ratio for Greenway is as follows:

| | 2009 £'000 | 2008 £'000 |
|---|---|---|
| Closing inventory | 2,410 | 2,000 |
| Cost of sales for year | 11,210 | 11,200 |
| One days cost of sales | 30.7 | 30.7 |
| Closing inventory/1 days cost of sales | 78.5 days | 65.1 days |

The conclusions we make from the inventory days ratio are exactly the same as the ones from the inventory turnover ratio, albeit that in general terms the lower the inventory days the more efficiently the entity is managing its inventory.

## 4.3 Trade receivables

The ratio we use to assess the 'real' level of trade receivables is the trade receivables day's ratio. It is computed in the same manner as the inventory day's ratio computed in 4.2 above and it is the ratio of closing trade receivables to 1 day's revenue. The ratio for Greenway is as follows:

|  | 2009 £'000 | 2008 £'000 |
|---|---|---|
| Closing trade receivables | 2,020 | 1,700 |
| Revenue for year | 14,310 | 14,500 |
| One day's revenue | 39.2 | 39.7 |
| Closing trade receivables /1 day's revenue | 51.5 days | 42.8 days |

In most circumstances an increase in this ratio means that the trade receivables are taking longer to collect. This could in turn increase the risk of customers failing to honour their obligations, leading to the need to write off or at least impair some of the trade receivables balance in the future. As stated in 4.2 above regarding inventory If we are interpreting audited financial statements we should have reasonable assurance that the trade receivables balance does not need to be written down for impairment. However if the financial statements are stated to be 'draft' or 'unaudited' it might be necessary to query the carrying value of the trade receivables balance  in the financial statements.

Other factors to bear in mind when interpreting this ratio are that:

■ trade receivables often include applicable sales taxes whereas revenue does not. Therefore in order to compute a strictly accurate ratio the sales tax included in the trade receivables number should be removed for the purposes of computing the ratio

■ the ratio matches closing trade receivables to revenue for the whole period. If the revenue is subject to significant seasonal variation then the ratio could be misstated.

Both the above issues are mitigated to some extent by the fact that when we are interpreting financial statements using ratio analysis we are comparing ratios from one period to another or from one entity to another. If the trade receivables days ratio is consistently computed using trade receivables that include sales taxes then the distortion is removed on comparison. The same could apply to seasonality factors.

## 4.4 Trade payables

When assessing the 'real' level of trade payables the ratio that would be most useful in theory is closing trade payables/one day's purchases (both included in cost of sales and in other operating expenses). This gives us a problem when using published financial data because the overall purchases number is not available.

Some analysts arrive at a 'proxy' number by computing total operating costs (including cost of sales) and adjusting for movements in inventory, depreciation, and staff costs. A more straightforward approach, and one that is usually perfectly acceptable in examinations, is to use total cost of sales as a 'proxy' for total purchases. The two numbers are most unlikely to be the same but given that we are comparing two ratios this technique will usually give us a reasonable assessment of the trend in the real level of trade payables. The calculation of the 'proxy ratio' is as follows:

|  | 2009 £'000 | 2008 £'000 |
| --- | --- | --- |
| Closing trade payables | 1,610 | 1,890 |
| Cost of sales for year | 11,210 | 11,200 |
| One days cost of sales | 30.7 | 30.7 |
| Closing trade payables/1 days cost of sales | 52.4 days | 61.6 days |

It is slightly more difficult to state whether a fall in this ratio is a good thing or not. Certainly if the ratio is too high then this could indicate the entity is having difficulty meeting its obligations which could in turn raise liquidity concerns. However reducing the ratio too far could mean we are paying our suppliers more quickly than we need to. This is unwise unless there are prompt payment discounts on offer.

In this case, of course we have information that would lead us to expect that the ratio would fall. We are told that Greenway has agreed to pay its suppliers quicker in return for price reductions so this reduction can probably be explained in those terms.

## 5 The link between working capital management and liquidity.

In chapter 4 we saw that liquidity can be assessed using ratios but also by examining the statement of cash flows. The statement of cash flows for Greenway is as follows.

| | £'000 | £'000 |
|---|---|---|
| **Cash flows from operating activities** | | |
| Profit before taxation | 1,540 | |
| Adjustments for: | | |
| Depreciation | 280 | |
| Profit on sale of administrative offices | (500) | |
| Finance cost | 110 | |
| | 1,430 | |
| Increase in trade and other receivables | (320) | |
| Increase in inventories | (410) | |
| Decrease in trade payables | (280) | |
| Cash generated from operations | 420 | |
| Interest paid | (110) | |
| Income taxes paid | (370) | |
| *Net cash from operating activities* | | (60) |
| **Cash flows from investing activities** | | |
| Purchase of property, plant and equipment | (400) | |
| Proceeds from sale of administrative offices | 3,000 | |
| Net cash raised from investing activities | | 2,600 |
| **Cash flows from financing activities** | | |
| Proceeds from the issue of share capital | 20 | |
| Payment of long-term borrowings | (2,200) | |
| Dividends paid | (190) | |
| *Net cash used in financing activities* | | (2,370) |

| | |
|---|---|
| **Net increase in cash and cash equivalents** | 170 |
| **Cash and cash equivalents at beginning of period** | 30 |
| **Cash and cash equivalents at end of period** | 200 |

It can be seen from the above statement that the profit before tax is (in £'000) 1,540 but the cash generated from operations before tax is (in £'000) only 310 (370 – 60). This equates to a difference (in £'000) of 1,230. Of this amount 1,010 (320 + 410 + 280) is due to an increase in working capital. Inventories and trade receivables have increased whilst trade payables have decreased. Entities that find it difficult to control their working capital levels often experience liquidity problems even when reporting reasonable levels of profit.

## 6 The link between the profitability ratios (the 'ratio pyramid')

Having basically computed all the profitability ratios we are now in a position to summarise the links between them in the 'ratio pyramid' as shown below:

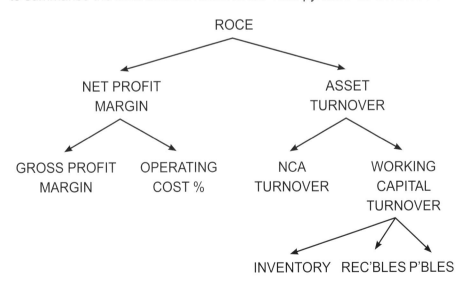

Appreciating this link between the profitability ratios can often be a very effective method of generating a logical 'flow' to profitability analysis.

## Chapter summary

■ One of the key factors that determine the profitability of an entity is the efficiency with which it utilises its capital. This overall efficiency is measured by the asset turnover ratio.

■ The asset turnover ratio is further assessed by sub-dividing the ratio into two constituent parts, non-current asset turnover and working capital turnover.

■ Working capital turnover is capable of being further broken down into three sub-ratios, inventory turnover (or inventory days), trade receivables days, and trade payables days. Each one of these ratios measures the 'real' level of the particular component of working capital

■ There is a clear link between working capital levels and liquidity. Entities that are unable to control their working capital levels tend to suffer from cash shortages.

■ All the profitability ratios can be linked together though the 'ratio pyramid'.

# Chapter 6

# Investor based analysis and non-financial analysis

## 1 Objectives of the chapter

**Having read this chapter you should be able to:**

- discuss the difference between entity and investor based analysis

- compute the main ratios that assist in investor based analysis

- describe the main components of a corporate report

- discuss the increasing trend towards non-financial performance measurement.

## 2 The difference between entity and investor based analysis

Chapters 3-5 of this book have described the key financial ratios that are used to assess the performance of an entity. In each of those chapters the focus of the analysis has been the business being analysed. An alternative perspective is to focus on the return available to the investors in the entity. In practice this usually involves considering the equity investors. Whilst many of the numbers used are the same as those used when focusing on the entity perspective the analysis does have a different emphasis. In practice investor based analysis moves from an initial focus on the financial numbers generated from the financial statements of the entity (non-market based analysis) to include a focus on the market value of the shares of entities that are listed (market based analysis).

## 2.1 The underlying financial information to be used in this chapter

The data that is relevant to this chapter is reproduced below, together with some additional market based information.

**1. Greenway plc – income statement for the year ended 30 September**

|  | Year ended 30 Sept 2009 | Year ended 30 Sept 2008 |
|---|---|---|
|  | £'000 | £'000 |
| Revenue | 14,310 | 14,500 |
| Cost of sales | (11,210) | (11,200) |
| Gross profit | 3,100 | 3,300 |
| Operating expenses | (1,350) | (1,100) |
| Non-recurring items (see note 1) | (100) | (400) |
| Profit from operations | 1,650 | 1,800 |
| Finance costs | (110) | (240) |
| Profit before taxation | 1,540 | 1,560 |
| Income tax | (330) | (470) |
| Profit for the period | 1,210 | 1,090 |
| **EPS** | 60.5p | 54.9p |

## 2. Greenway plc - statement of financial position at 30 September

| | At 30 Sept 2009 | | At 30 Sept 2008 | |
|---|---|---|---|---|
| | £'000 | £'000 | £'000 | £'000 |
| **ASSETS** | | | | |
| **Non-current assets** | | | | |
| Property, plant & equipment | | 3,620 | | 6,000 |
| **Current assets** | | | | |
| Inventories | 2,410 | | 2,000 | |
| Trade and other receivables | 2,020 | | 1,700 | |
| Cash and cash equivalents | 200 | | 30 | |
| | | 4,630 | | 3,730 |
| **Total assets** | | 8,250 | | 9,730 |
| **EQUITY & LIABILITIES** | | | | |
| **Equity** | | | | |
| Issued capital - £1 ordinary shares | | 2,010 | | 1,990 |
| Retained earnings | | 1,170 | | 150 |
| | | 3,180 | | 2,140 |
| **Non-current liabilities** | | | | |
| Borrowings | | 3,300 | | 5,500 |
| **Current liabilities** | | | | |
| Trade payables | 1,610 | | 1,890 | |
| Other payables | 160 | | 200 | |
| | | 1,770 | | 2,090 |
| **Total equity and liabilities** | | 8,250 | | 9,730 |

## 3. Greenway plc – other information

| | 2009 | 2008 |
|---|---|---|
| Weighted average number of shares in issue ('000s) | 2,000 | 1985 |
| Dividend paid in period (£'000s) | 190 | 180 |
| Share price at end of period | £3.05 | £2.50 |

# 3 The main ratios that assist in investor based analysis

## 3.1 Earnings per share (EPS)

EPS is essentially an investor based profitability ratio. It is the ratio of profits attributable to the equity shareholders to the weighted average number of equity shares in issue during the financial year. For Greenway EPS is already given but the calculation can be proved as follows:

| | 2009 £'000 | 2008 £'000 |
|---|---|---|
| Profits attributable to the equity shareholders | 1,210 | 1,090 |
| Weighted average number of equity shares in issue | 2,000 | 1985 |
| So EPS (in pence) equals | 60.5 | 54.9 |

The trend in EPS over the two years is increasing which is a positive sign. It is effectively a profitability ratio and the rising trend reflects the underlying increase in profitability we discussed in chapter 3. Therefore when using EPS as an interpretation tool the reasons for a change in EPS will often be related to changes in underlying profitability. Other reasons for a change in EPS could include:

■ an issue of shares at other than full market price. This could be a rights issue or a bonus issue (a bonus issue is an issue of shares for no cash consideration from the shareholders, perhaps as a 'dividend in kind'). In either circumstance an increase in the number of shares in issue would not necessarily lead to a corresponding increase in reported profits

■ a 'lag' between an additional equity investment by the shareholders and the investment of the additional funds generated in profitable projects.

## 3.2 Dividend cover

Dividend cover measures the relationship between profits attributable to the equity shareholders and the dividend actually paid or declared in the period. The calculation is relatively straightforward:

|  | 2009 £'000 | 2008 £'000 |
|---|---|---|
| Profits attributable to the equity shareholders | 1,210 | 1,090 |
| Dividend paid | 190 | 180 |
| So dividend cover equals | 6.4 times | 6.1 times |

Essentially the dividend cover measures the 'security' of the dividend payment. Whilst strictly speaking the amount of legally distributable profits is based on the cumulative balance in retained earnings rather than the profits for a single period most entities would be reluctant to pay a dividend which is larger than the most recently computed profits. Therefore if the dividend cover ratio is low this could mean that the dividend might be reduced in future periods. The higher is the dividend cover the less likely it is that this will happen. Does this mean, therefore, that the shareholders of Greenway will be happy that the dividend cover has increased from 6.1 to 6.4? Not necessarily, because a high dividend cover indicates that a relatively low proportion of profit is being paid out as a dividend and the shareholders might feel that a larger payment is appropriate. It is difficult to identify exact figures but once the dividend cover is well above one, as it certainly is for Greenway, the shareholders might prefer the cover to be lowered by an increased dividend.

In this particular situation it may be that the dividend cover is relatively high because Greenway has apparently been making losses in periods prior to 2008. The retained earnings at 31 March 2008 were £150,000 and the profit for the year ended 31 March 2008 was £1.09 million. Therefore, at the start of 2007/08 there were negative retained earnings. In such circumstances it is perhaps understandable that the management of Greenway are adopting a cautious approach to dividend payouts.

## 3.3 Dividend yield

Both the EPS and the dividend cover are non-market based investor ratios. This is because neither ratio relates performance to the market price of the share. For listed entities (for whom share prices are readily available) it is also possible to compute market based ratios, of which dividend yield is one. The dividend yield is the ratio of the dividend per share to the listed (or market) price of the share and it is expressed as a percentage. For Greenway, the relevant calculations are as follows:

| | 2009 | 2008 |
|---|---|---|
| Dividend (£'000) | 190 | 180 |
| Number of equity shares in issue ('000) | 2,010 | 1,990 |
| Dividend per share (pence) | 9.5 pence | 9.1 pence |
| Listed price of the equity shares (pence) | 305 pence | 250 pence |
| So dividend yield equals | 3.1% | 3.6% |

For a listed entity, you could argue that the dividend yield represents the return on the effective investment by the shareholders (because the shareholders could sell their shares at listed price, so choosing to retain them means they have effectively invested the latest listed price in the entity). Based on this argument, you would argue that the shareholders are less content in 2009 that they were in 2008 because the dividend yield has fallen. Part of the reason for this may be the apparently cautious dividend policy due to losses in periods prior to 2007/08. However we should also remember that a fall in dividend yield could be caused by two somewhat conflicting factors:

■ a fall in the 'effective' dividend – not a positive sign for the shareholders perhaps

■ a rise in the listed price of the share – which increases shareholder wealth and would almost certainly be regarded as a good thing for the shareholders.

This means that we must interpret changes in 'market-based' ratios with caution. A final factor to mention when interpreting ratios of this kind is that changes in listed prices could be due either to the market's perception of the performance of the particular entity (a 'specific' factor) or to general economic trends (a 'general' factor). If the data is available, analysts often investigate changes in a particular share price relative to general market trends. Unfortunately, for Greenway, we do not have this information.

## 3.4 The Price Earnings (PE) ratio

The PE ratio is another market based measure as it relates the share price to the underlying earnings. For Greenway the ratio is:

|  | 2009 | 2008 |
| --- | --- | --- |
| Listed price of the equity shares (pence) | 305 pence | 250 pence |
| Earnings per share (pence) | 60.5 pence | 54.9 pence |
| So PE ratio equals | 5.0 | 4.6 |

The PE ratio of an entity measures the number of years' earnings that the listed price represents. On the whole the higher the PE ratio the higher is the market perception of the relevant entity. The rise here is probably good news and could have been caused by the fact that by the end of 2008/09 Greenway had shown at least 2 years of reasonable profits and the market was expecting this to continue into 2009/10 and beyond. However with any 'market base' ratio we must remember that changes could be cause by general market conditions as well as 'company specific factors'.

All in all, interpretation of 'market-based' ratios must be performed with great caution.

# 4 The main components of a corporate report

A typical annual report layout for a listed entity would be as follows:

## 4.1 The chief executive's statement – often containing financial highlights

The title of this statement perfectly describes its function. It is not subject to regulation or audit and so analysts tend to treat its contents with caution. However it can contain some useful information about the intentions of management regarding the future of the business and so should not be ignored completely.

## 4.2 The business review

The business review of a listed entity must include, to the extent necessary for an understanding of the development, performance or position of the entity's business.

- The main trends and factors likely to affect the future development, performance and position of the entity's business.

- Information about environmental matters, the entity's employees, and social and community issues, including information about the entity's policies on these issues and their effectiveness.

- Information about persons with whom the entity has contractual or other arrangements essential to the entity's business, unless disclosure would in the directors' opinion seriously prejudice that person and be contrary to the public interest.

The government has stated that entities will not be required to list their suppliers and customers, or to provide detail about contracts, but they will have to report significant relationships likely to influence, directly or indirectly, the business's performance and value.

Entities are exempted from disclosing information about impending developments or matters in the course of negotiation where disclosure would in the directors' opinion be seriously prejudicial to the entity's interests.

The contents of the business review are regulated in the UK by the 2006 Companies Act and some of the non-financial information in particular might be of relevance to certain users. For example, information about environmental matters is likely to be increasingly sought due to the higher profile generally being given to 'green' issues.

## 4.3 Information concerning directors and their responsibilities – corporate governance matters

Listed UK entities are required to prepare a remuneration report that provides background on the remuneration of directors and provides information about the way in which the entity is governed.

The remuneration report must disclose salaries, fees, bonuses, expenses, compensation for loss of office and other benefits paid to a director. The legislation is worded to ensure that payments made to a director in any form are included, preventing surreptitious bonuses or benefits. The report must also disclose information relating to pension payments. For defined benefit schemes changes in accrued benefit, the transfer value and the amount obtained (the current transfer value minus last year's transfer value and any contributions made by the individual) must be disclosed. Therefore, one may assess the benefit obtained under the scheme and the cost to the company. This is especially important for defined benefit schemes, as the cost of these schemes to entities has increased public scrutiny recently.

The Combined Code on Corporate Governance sets out standards of good practice in relation to issues such as board composition and development, remuneration, accountability and audit and relations with shareholders. All UK listed entities are required under the Listing Rules to report on how they have applied the Combined Code in their annual report and accounts. The Combined Code contains broad principles and more specific provisions. Listed entities are required to report on how they have applied the main principles of the Code, and either to confirm that they have complied with the Code's provisions or - where they have not - to provide an explanation.

## 4.4 The directors' report

The accounts must include a directors' report which includes:

- the names of the persons who, at any time of the financial year, were directors of the entity

- the principal activities of the company

- a business review – see 4.2 above.

The directors' report must also contain a statement to the effect that, in the case of each of the persons who are directors at the time the report is approved, so far as the directors are aware, there is no relevant audit information of which the entity's auditor is unaware, and he has taken all the steps he ought to have taken as a director in order to make himself aware of any relevant audit information and to establish that the entity's auditor is aware of that information.

## 4.5 The auditors' report

The auditors' report is a report to the shareholders of the entity that provides them with assurance regarding the truth and fairness of the financial statements (see 4.6 below). The report also sets out the responsibilities of the directors (to prepare financial statements that give a true and fair view) and of the auditors (to report on those statements).

## 4.6 The financial statements

These have been our focus in the book so far and these are the usually what is provided (in whole or in part) in examination questions. Analysts tend to focus more on the financial statements than the rest of the corporate report because of the fact that they are regulated and audited.

# 5 Non-financial performance measurement

Despite the tendency for analysts to focus on financial measures of performance it is nevertheless true that non-financial analysis is carried out, particularly for users other than shareholders. For example, if we consider the information needs of employees they are probably focused around issues such as:

- long term job security

- the entity's interaction with the local community

- the entity's environmental policies.

This type of information is not fully captured by financial measures on their own and so such users might well refer to the business review (see 4.2 above) to obtain such information.

An additional need for non-financial information is present when the entity does not have financial objectives as its only key objectives. For example a hospital does have financial criteria by which it is judged but clearly from the point of view of patients and their families the quality of the care provided is far more important than the financial position of the hospital.

A problem frequently encountered with non-financial performance measures is to devise a suitable method of measuring performance. Non-financial performance indicators tend to be more specific to the type of entity. For example a non-financial performance indicator for a school might be the examination results of its students, whereas for a hospital it could be the 'success' of a surgical procedure.

# Chapter summary

■ Investor ratios focus on the position of the investor, rather than the entity. The investor ratios are divided into non-market and market based ratios.

■ The two non-market based ratios are earnings per share and dividend cover.

■ The two market based ratios are dividend yield and price earnings ratio.

■ A corporate report for a listed entity contains a number of documents other than the financial statements. Some useful non-financial information can often be found in the business review.

■ Non-financial performance indicators are particularly useful for certain types of users in all entities (e.g. employees) and for entities where many of the key objectives are non-financial (e.g. schools and hospitals).

# Chapter 7

## Case study

## 1 Objectives of the chapter

**Having read this chapter you should be able to:**

■ apply the principles we have covered in the previous six chapters to a practical scenario that you might encounter in your examination.

## 2 Overall approach to financial analysis questions

1. Check the exact requirements that are indicated in the question.

2. Read all the information that is given and consider the potential implications for financial analysis – e.g. the type of entity being analysed, unusual transactions in the period, changes in accounting policies or accounting estimates etc.

3. Review the financial statements as a whole and consider what the major differences are between the current year financial statements and the benchmark of comparison (which could be, for example, last year's financial statements or the financial statements of another, comparable, entity).

4. If the question specifically asks you to calculate certain ratios then do so. If not then go to step 5.

5. Compute the accounting ratios that are relevant to the key differences.

6. Consider reasons for the variations in the ratios you have calculated.

7. Write your answer in a report format.

## 3 Case study question

### 3.1 Question 1 from the ICAEW Financial Reporting examination for September 2009

Stavros is a chartered accountant employed by Fuller Cards Ltd (Fuller), an unlisted company that sells greetings cards, gift wrap and small gifts from its retail shops throughout the UK. Fuller's managing director, Luigi, has asked Stavros to analyse and report on some information relating to one of Fuller's competitors, Primavella Cards plc (Primavella), a UK listed company.

Primavella's share of the UK greetings card market is estimated at 7%; Fuller's share is about 3-4%. When handing over the information to Stavros, Luigi said: 'Primavella's managing director approached me a few months ago to ask if Fuller would be interested in acquiring a few of their shops. I declined the offer, because I suspected that they were trying to dispose of their least profitable shops. Incidentally, can you explain to me the significance of the line "Non-current assets held for sale"? Surely, an asset is either sold or not sold?'

**Extract from interview with Primavella's finance director (reported in the trade press in November 2008)**

'We are looking forward to a successful Christmas which, for all card retailers, is one of the most important sales periods in the year. However, the recession is likely to have a severe adverse impact on retail businesses in 2009 and 2010. Therefore, we have been using some of our cash surplus to repay certain long term borrowings before they fall due. We also have plans to rationalise our network of shops. In a recession, people continue to buy cards and presents to celebrate important occasions, but typically they spend less on average. We have therefore decided to introduce a new budget range of cards and gift wrap in January 2009'.

**Primavella Cards plc – Income statement for the year ended 31 March:**

|  | 2009 £m | 2008 £m |
|---|---|---|
| Revenue | 103.7 | 108.9 |
| Cost of sales (see note below) | (97.3) | (96.8) |
| Gross profit | 6.4 | 12.1 |
| Other costs | (3.6) | (3.2) |
| Profit from operations | 2.8 | 8.9 |
| Finance costs less finance income | (0.8) | (0.7) |
| Profit before tax | 2.0 | 8.2 |
| Tax | (0.5) | (2.1) |
| Profit after tax | **1.5** | **6.1** |
| Earnings per share | **30p** | **122p** |

## Notes

■ A dividend of £1.0 million (2008: £1.5 million) was proposed and paid during the financial year ended 31 March 2009.

■ Cost of sales for the year ended 31 March 2009 included impairment losses of £3 million (2008: £nil).

# Primavella Cards plc – Statement of financial position as at 31 March

|  | 2009 | | 2008 | |
| --- | --- | --- | --- | --- |
|  | £m | £m | £m | £m |
| **ASSETS** | | | | |
| **Non-current assets** | | | | |
| Property, plant & equipment | | 36.6 | | 43.7 |
| **Current assets** | | | | |
| Inventories | 9.8 | | 8.9 | |
| Sundry receivables and prepayments | 0.7 | | 0.6 | |
| Cash and cash equivalents | 2.7 | | 7.8 | |
| | | 13.2 | | 17.3 |
| **Non-current assets held for sale** | | 3.3 | | - |
| **Total assets** | | 53.1 | | 61.0 |
| | | | | |
| **EQUITY AND LIABILITIES** | | | | |
| **Capital and reserves** | | | | |
| Issued capital - £1 ordinary shares | | 5.0 | | 5.0 |
| Share premium | | 1.7 | | 1.7 |
| Retained earnings | | 15.6 | | 15.1 |
| Equity | | 22.3 | | 21.8 |
| **Non-current liabilities** | | | | |
| Long-term borrowings | | 8.7 | | 16.9 |
| **Current liabilities** | | | | |
| Trade and other payables | 21.3 | | 19.9 | |
| Taxation | 0.5 | | 2.1 | |
| Short-term borrowings | 0.3 | | 0.3 | |
| | | 22.1 | | 22.3 |
| **Total equity and liabilities** | | 53.1 | | 61.0 |

## Additional information about Primavella

|  | 2009 | 2008 |
|---|---|---|
| Number of shops at year-end (approximately half of the premises are owned by Primavella; the rest are held on short-term leases) | 263 | 266 |
| Average revenue per square metre of retail premises | £1,971 | £2,047 |
| Gross profit margin | 6.2% | 11.1% |
| Gearing (net debt/equity) | 28.3% | 43.1% |
| Cash from operations/profit from operations | 275% | 135% |
| Return on capital employed | 9.8% | 28.8% |

### Requirements

Write a report to the managing director that:

(a) Explains the significance of the separate presentation of 'non-current assets held for sale' in the statement of financial position; and **(3 marks)**

(b) Analyses the financial performance and position of Primavella Cards plc. Your report should include the calculation of a maximum of five additional relevant ratios, and should identify and justify matters that you consider require further investigation. **(18 marks)**

**(21 marks)**

# 4 Outline of approach to the question

## 4.1 Overall review of requirements

In this case the first requirement is a fairly 'closed' financial reporting 'knowledge' requirement. Non-current assets held for sale are defined in IFRS 5 – Non-current assets held for sale and discontinued operations. They are assets or business units whose value will primarily be recovered through sale rather than through continued use. IFRS 5 contains further guidance criteria to 'flesh out' this basic concept.

Non-current assets held for sale are removed from non-current assets from their date of classification. IFRS 5 allows them to be shown within current assets or (as is done in this case study) as a separate line in the statement of financial position. Such assets are only depreciated up to the date of classification. Their carrying value at the date of classification is compared with the expected net selling price (described in IFRS 5 as 'Fair value less costs to sell'). If fair value less costs to sell is less than current carrying value then the asset (or business unit) is written down to fair value less costs to sell and the reduction reported as an impairment loss in accordance with IAS 36 – Impairment of assets. It would be misleading to leave such assets in non-current assets given the change of management intention regarding future use.

The key requirement here that can be used to demonstrate the principles explained in this book is the second requirement. We are asked to report on the financial performance and financial position of Primavella and to compute a maximum of five additional ratios to assist us – clearly some must have been given. As we read the information thoroughly we should consider the additional ratios that are likely to be of most benefit to assist us in this review that we are not given already.

## 4.2 Thorough read of all the information that is given

■ Primavella is a retailer of cards – a seasonal business. It has been affected by the recession.

■ Primavella is introducing a 'budget' range of cards. This is likely to affect profit margins. The company also has plans to rationalise its shops.

■ Profits and dividends are reduced compared with last year.

■ Cost of sales includes an impairment loss. This could be connected with the classification of some assets as held for sale (see 4.1 above).

■ The statement of financial position shows that the entity has less cash at the end of the year than at the start.

■ The profitability ratios do not look good. Further investigation is needed. It would be useful to compute additional profitability ratios.

■ The ratio of sales to square metre of floor space – a key 'sector specific' ratio – is reduced. The decision to introduce a 'budget' range of cards could have had some impact on this ratio although the new range only starts from January 2009 – three months prior to the year-end.

## 4.3 Review of the financial statements as a whole

■ Revenues have reduced and cost of sales has increased. This is bound to have a negative impact on the gross profit margin.

■ Other operating costs have increased from £3.2m to £3.6m. This will place severe pressure on the operating profit margin.

■ There is a reduction in non-current assets, which is consistent with the policy of store sales.

■ Inventories have increased in a period of declining revenues. This is slightly surprising. It is worth computing the inventory days ratio.

■ There is a reduction in cash balances but this is less than the reduction in long-term borrowings. We are told these have been reduced. This must mean that the company has generated cash from its operations to partly finance this difference. [In fact the question tells us that operating cash flow is 275% of operating profit so operating cash flow must have been £7.7m (£2.8m x 2.75). However this is less than the operating cash flow in 2008 which was £12m (£8.9m x 1.35)

# 4.4 Calculation of five additional ratios

There are a number that you can choose from:

## 1. Operating profit margin

|  | 2009 | 2008 |
|---|---|---|
|  | £m | £m |
| Profit from operations | 2.8 | 8.9 |
| Revenue | 103.7 | 108.9 |
| **So profit margin equals** | **2.7%** | **8.2%** |

## 2. Asset turnover

|  | 2009 | 2008 |
|---|---|---|
|  | £m | £m |
| Revenue | 103.7 | 108.9 |
| Capital employed (see below) | 28.6 | 31.2 |
| **So asset turnover equals** | **3.6 times** | **3.5 times** |

### Working – capital employed

|  | 2009 | 2008 |
|---|---|---|
|  | £m | £m |
| Equity | 22.3 | 21.8 |
| Long term borrowings | 8.7 | 16.9 |
| Short term borrowings | 0.3 | 0.3 |
| Cash and cash equivalents | (2.7) | (7.8) |
|  | 28.6 | 31.2 |

Note that there are a number of possible methods of computing borrowings. In this case they are taken as the sum of short term and long term less cash and cash equivalents. Other versions would have been acceptable.

## 3. Inventory days

|  | 2009 | 2008 |
|---|---|---|
|  | £m | £m |
| Closing inventory | 9.8 | 8.9 |
| Cost of sales | 97.3 | 96.8 |
| 1 days cost of sales | 0.27 | 0.27 |
| **So inventory days are** | **36 days** | **33 days** |

## 4. Current ratio

|  | 2009 | 2008 |
|---|---|---|
|  | £m | £m |
| Current assets | 13.2 | 17.3 |
| Current liabilities | 22.1 | 22.3 |
| **So current ratio equals** | **0.60** | **0.78** |

## 5. Interest cover

|  | 2009 | 2008 |
|---|---|---|
|  | £m | £m |
| Profit from operations | 2.8 | 8.9 |
| Net finance cost | 0.8 | 0.7 |
| **So interest cover equals** | **3.5 times** | **12.7 times** |

Other ratios could equally have been computed but in a question like this you would not compute more than five given the very specific requirements in the question.

## 4.5 Compute accounting ratios that are relevant to the key differences

In a question of this format this step is not necessary as an appropriate number of ratios has either been given or computed already.

## 4.6 Consideration of reasons for the variations in the calculated ratios

This should be done taking into account the context that the question provides. It is clear in this question that there has been a significant deterioration in profitability as measured by the return on capital employed. A key cause of this deterioration is a significant decline in both gross and net profit margins. This may have been due to the decision to introduce a budget range of cards but some of it is also caused by the impairment charge. In fact if we were to compute the gross profit margin for 2009 after reversing out the impairment loss we would get 9.1% [ (6.4 + 3.0)/103.7] compared with the 2008 figure of 11.1%. This is still a significant decline but not as marked as before.

A noteworthy feature of the change in financial position is the reduction in the gearing ratio that is cause by the repayment of borrowings. This has caused the current ratio to decline but given the extent of the repayment of borrowings this may not be of great concern. We would also comment on the increase in inventory days, this could possibly be caused by the introduction of the new 'budget' range.

## 4.7 Answer in a report format

A sample report appears below:

**Report**
To: Luigi, Managing director
From:   Stavros, Accountant
7 September 2009

**Primavella Cards plc: analysis of information relating to the financial year ended 31 March 2009**

**Financial performance**

Primavella has experienced a significant decline in profitability as measured by the return on capital employed. The financial statements show that revenue has decreased by 4.8% in the financial year ended 31 March 2009. The fall in the number of shops suggests that there has been a reduction in activity over the year. Average revenue per square metre of space has fallen by 3.7%, which may suggest that price cutting has taken place, or that the more economical product lines have been selling better than high margin goods. The introduction of the budget range may partly explain this trend although this did not occur until January 2009 so this may have had limited effect on the overall figures and trends

The effect of the reduction in activity on profitability has been very marked indeed: gross, operating and net margins are substantially reduced. Even after excluding the effects of the impairment loss, the reduction in margins is significant. However, if Primavella's introduction of a budget range of goods proves to be successful, the adverse effects of the general economic downturn could be mitigated.

Interest cover has fallen from 12.7 to 3.5. However, this ratio has had to be calculated using a net figure of finance costs less finance income. It would be preferable to split the figure into its component parts in order to be able to assess the true impact of finance costs. Net interest costs have increased in the year despite a reduction in the amount of debt held at the end of the reporting period. This could be due to the debt being repaid towards the end of the reporting period.

## Financial position

The statement of financial position at 31 March 2009 suggests some contraction in activities. The carrying amount of property, plant and equipment has fallen by 16.2%. However, this is partly due to the separate presentation of non-current assets held for sale. Also at least part, if not all, of the impairment loss is likely to be attributable to a fall in the value of non-current assets. It is not clear from the information given whether or not some of the non-current assets have already been disposed of. It is not possible to tell whether or not the number of shops at the year-end includes any shops held for sale. More information is required in this respect.

The long-term borrowings figure has almost halved from £16.9 million to £8.7 million, which will reduce the burden of interest payments in the future. This appears to be a prudent move in conditions of increasing pressure on profitability. There has been a sizeable reduction in cash, too, although the amount of £2.7m remaining at 31 March 2009 is substantial, and certainly adequate for immediate needs.

Although the quality of earnings, as indicated by cash from operations as a percentage of profit from operations, is good and improving (it has increased from 135% to 275%) given the reduction in operating profits between 2009 and 2008 there is less cash generated from operations in 2009 than in 2008. Primavella's inventory days have increased slightly from 33.6 to 36.8 days, but the turnover rate remains rapid. The small increase could be attributable to the introduction of the additional budget line of goods, especially if other lines have remained at their previous levels. More information on this point would be useful; some regular visits to the Primavella shops could provide useful evidence of their trading policies.

The current ratio has fallen significantly from 0.78:1 to 0.60:1 but the sale of the non-current assets held for sale of £3.3 million will provide a significant cash flow advantage after the year-end, and the ratio could return to more normal levels.

## Matters requiring further investigation

The information provided about non-current assets is limited. It would be helpful to know more about the short leasehold arrangements in order to gauge their flexibility. No information has been provided about rates of depreciation, or about acquisitions and disposals of noncurrent assets that have taken place in the year. It is possible, for example, that refitting and updating of premises has been delayed in order to save cash.

Very little can be discerned about cash movements during the year from the information provided. It would be helpful to have a statement of cash flows to determine inflows and outflows relating to such items as repayments of borrowings, and acquisitions and disposals of non-current assets.

The information about Primavella would be enhanced by industry comparatives, especially those relating to other listed companies involved in greetings card retailing. This would allow comparison of key ratios such as revenue per square metre.

## Chapter summary

- The report that has been produced above is not totally comprehensive. It is based around the analytical work that has actually been performed. It is worth noting that the report:

- is provided in accordance with the requirements of the question

- is not 'overloaded' with figures

- attempts to explain movements in ratios etc. rather than just saying they have gone up or down

- takes full account of the information provided in the question regarding the general context.

- You should follow this approach when attempting the practice questions that are included in chapter 8.

# Chapter 8

## Illustrative questions and answers

This chapter contains seven past examination questions. You should attempt to answer each one using the framework we developed in chapter 7. Suggested answers are provided at the end of the chapter.

Please note that these questions follow the same conventions as the relevant examining body in terms of the use of £ or $ signs.

# 1 Question one

## ICAEW – Financial Reporting – March 2009

1. Mossylea Ltd (Mossylea) is a wholly owned subsidiary of Fructose plc (Fructose). Mossylea prepares its financial statements in accordance with IFRS. Fructose has decided to dispose of its investment in Mossylea. Mossylea manufactures bread and bakery products.

   You are an accountant at Orrell plc (Orrell). The managing director of Orrell has presented you with some financial information for Mossylea for the year ended 31 December 2008 and said:

   "I'm interested in Orrell acquiring Mossylea. I'd like you to spend some time analysing these financial statements. I'm particularly interested in Mossylea's financial performance and financial position (including liquidity and solvency). I've sent you some notes that I believe are important. Please send me a report that documents your review and conclusions. I will use it to develop my thinking."

### Mossylea Ltd – Key matters during the year ended 31 December 2008

■ Selling prices to third parties for bread and bakery products have increased by over 7% in the last year. A significant proportion of revenue is generated by selling to Fructose.

■ Purchase prices of raw materials such as flour have risen by 12% during the year and are still rising, partly due to a drought in Australia. All raw material purchases are from unconnected third parties.

■ Heat, light and power costs have increased substantially year on year.

■ Fructose charges Mossylea annually for management services it provides to Mossylea.

■ New manufacturing equipment costing over £1 million was installed in November 2007.

■ An additional range of products was launched in March 2008 which have not proved popular with customers.

■ All of Mossylea's debt finance is provided by Fructose.

■ A taxation investigation was completed during 2008 and £200,000 of additional taxation in respect of prior years was paid.

**Mossylea Ltd - income statement for the year ended 31 December 2008**

| | Year ended 31 Dec 2008 | Year ended 31 Dec 2007 |
|---|---|---|
| | £'000 | £'000 |
| Revenue (see note 1) | 9,730 | 8,900 |
| Cost of sales | (7,600) | (6,930) |
| Gross profit | 2,130 | 1,970 |
| Operating expenses | (830) | (810) |
| Management charge (see note 1) | (500) | (1,000) |
| Profit from operations | 800 | 160 |
| Finance costs (see note 1) | (50) | (50) |
| Profit before taxation | 750 | 110 |
| Income tax | (430) | (30) |
| Profit after taxation | 320 | 80 |

No dividends have been paid or proposed.

# Mossylea Ltd - Statement of Financial Position at 31 December 2008

| | At 31 Dec 2008 | | At 31 Dec 2007 | |
|---|---|---|---|---|
| | £'000 | £'000 | £'000 | £'000 |
| **ASSETS** | | | | |
| **Non-current assets** | | | | |
| Property, plant & equipment | | 3,700 | | 3,430 |
| | | | | |
| **Current assets** | | | | |
| Inventories | 490 | | 460 | |
| Trade and other receivables | 1,110 | | 1,150 | |
| Cash and cash equivalents | 70 | | 50 | |
| | | 1,670 | | 1,660 |
| **Total assets** | | 5,370 | | 5,090 |
| | | | | |
| **EQUITY & LIABILITIES** | | | | |
| **Capital & reserves** | | | | |
| Issued capital - £1 ordinary shares | | 1,800 | | 1,800 |
| Retained earnings | | (820) | | (1,140) |
| Equity | | 980 | | 660 |
| | | | | |
| **Non-current liabilities** | | | | |
| 2% loan due to Fructose (see Note 1) | | 2,500 | | 2,500 |
| | | | | |
| **Current liabilities** | | | | |
| Trade and other payables | 1,840 | | 1,890 | |
| Taxation | 50 | | 40 | |
| | | 1,890 | | 1,930 |
| **Total equity and liabilities** | | 5,370 | | 5,090 |

## Note 1 - Related Party Transactions

During 2008 Mossylea recognised revenue of £1.0 million (2007 - £0.3 million) on sales to Fructose. Fructose made a management charge in 2008 of £0.5 million (2007 - £1.0 million) in respect of administrative and other operating services provided. The loan due to Fructose is repayable in 2012 and carries a fixed rate of interest of 2% per annum.

## Additional Information

|  | 2008 | 2007 |
|---|---|---|
| Operating margin | 8.2% | 1.8% |
| Industry average operating margin | 11.6% | 11.1% |
| Return on capital employed (ROCE) | 23.5% | 5.1% |
| EBITDA (£'000) | 1,580 | 1,390 |
| Ratio of capital expenditure to depreciation expense | 2.0 times | 5.0 times |

## Required

(a) Explain the usefulness of related party transaction disclosures when analysing financial performance and financial position. **(3 marks)**

(b) Analyse the given financial information for Mossylea as requested by the Managing Director, calculating a maximum of five additional relevant ratios to assist in your analysis. Your answer should identify and justify matters that you consider require further investigation. **(18 marks)**

**(21 marks)**

# 2 Question two

## ICAEW – Financial Reporting – June 2009

Trindac plc (Trindac) is a listed company which prepares its financial statements in accordance with IFRS. Trindac provides general waste management services to industry.

Following a long period of falling profit margins, Trindac's directors decided, early in 2008, to launch a takeover bid for Ensmarr plc (Ensmarr), a listed company that provides specialist waste management services to hospitals, an area in which Trindac had not previously operated. Ensmarr's year end is 31 December. Ensmarr experienced rapid growth in the years 2005 to 2007, while maintaining high levels of profitability over that period. Ensmarr's directors advised its shareholders to reject the bid, but by March 2008, Trindac had succeeded in gaining control, purchasing 60% of Ensmarr's ordinary share capital. Ensmarr's board of directors resigned in March 2008 and immediately established a competitor business.

Gloria Childs is a member of the family which originally established Trindac. Neither she, nor any other family member, has any active involvement in the business. Gloria holds 2% of the ordinary share capital of Trindac, and relies upon its dividends for a significant part of her income. She is concerned about the performance of Trindac for the year ended 31 December 2008.

Relevant extracts from the financial statements are as follows:

**Trindac plc – consolidated income statement for the year ended 31 December:**

|  | 2008 | 2007 |
|---|---|---|
|  | £m | £m |
| Revenue | 230.5 | 193.0 |
| Cost of sales | (204.0) | (169.0) |
| Gross profit | 26.5 | 24.0 |
| Other costs | (5.1) | (3.8) |
| Profit from operations | 21.4 | 20.2 |
| Finance costs | (13.7) | (9.1) |
| Profit before tax | 7.7 | 11.1 |
| Tax | (2.9) | (2.7) |
| Profit after tax | 4.8 | 8.4 |

**Trindac plc – consolidated statement of cash flows for the year ended 31 December:**

|  | 2008 £m | 2007 £m |
|---|---|---|
| Cash flows from operating activities | | |
| Cash generated from operations | 69.5 | 52.3 |
| Interest paid | (13.7) | (9.1) |
| Tax paid | (2.7) | (2.5) |
| Net cash from operating activities | 53.1 | 40.7 |
| Cash flows from investing activities | | |
| Purchase of property, plant and equipment | (52.1) | (40.4) |
| Purchase of investment in subsidiary | (60.0) | - |
| Net cash used in investing activities | (112.1) | (40.4) |
| Cash flows from financing activities | | |
| Dividends paid | (2.0) | (3.0) |
| Borrowings | 54.7 | 11.3 |
| Net cash from financing activities | 52.7 | 8.3 |
| Changes in cash and cash equivalents | (6.3) | 8.6 |

**Trindac plc – extracts from consolidated segment information for the year ended 31 December 2008:**

|  | General waste management £m | Specialist waste management £m |
|---|---|---|
| Revenue | 191.5 | 39.0 |
| Gross profit | 20.3 | 6.2 |
| Profit from operations | 16.2 | 5.2 |
| Finance costs | 12.8 | 0.9 |

**Additional information**

■ Trindac purchased its shareholding in Ensmarr for £60 million. Goodwill on acquisition was £31.8 million. In the annual report Trindac's managing director noted that the acquisition of Ensmarr 'brings great advantages to the group because of Ensmarr's skilled workforce and its respected position in the industry'.

■ The specialist waste segment comprises Ensmarr only. Ensmarr's last set of published financial statements prior to takeover showed a gross profit margin of 17.2% and an operating margin of 15.3%.

■ A dividend of 20p per share was paid during the 2008 financial year (2007: 30p). Issued ordinary share capital of Trindac was unchanged in 2007 and 2008 at £10.0 million.

|  | 2008 | 2007 |
|---|---|---|
| Equity at carrying amount | £152.5 million | £130.9 million |
| Net debt at carrying amount | £197.8 million | £122.6 million |
| Earnings per share | 39p | 84p |
| Price/earnings ratio | 11.7 | 14.9 |
| Interest cover | 1.56 | 2.22 |
| Receivables days | 57.2 | 57.9 |
| Payables days | 88.9 | 80.8 |
| Current ratio | 0.66 | 0.85 |
| Non-current asset turnover ratio | 0.63 | 0.74 |

## Requirements

(a) Explain the benefits and limitations of segment information reported under the requirements of IFRS 8, Operating Segments. **(5 marks)**

(b) Prepare a report for Gloria that analyses the financial performance and position of the group. Your report should include the calculation of a maximum of five additional relevant ratios, and should identify and justify matters that you consider require further investigation.

**(18 marks)**

**(23 marks)**

## 3 Question three

### CIMA F2 - Financial Management – Pilot Paper 2010

XYZ has a strategy of growth by acquisition. Two entities, A and B, have been identified and will be considered at the next board meeting. The target entities are of a similar size and operate within similar economic parameters. Neither entity is listed. The entities are subject to different tax regimes. Takeover is unlikely to be resisted by either entity, provided a reasonable price is offered for the shares.

XYZ can afford to fund only one acquisition and the board are asking for a review of the financial statements of both entities together with a recommendation on which of the entities looks a more promising prospect. In previous acquisitions, the board focused mainly on key benchmarks of profitability, efficiency and risk and to that end it is expecting any report to include analysis of the following key financial ratios:

■ gross profit percentage

■ profit before tax as a percentage of revenue

■ return on capital employed

■ non-current asset turnover

■ gearing (debt/equity).

The most recent income statements for both A and B are presented below, together with extracts from their statements of financial position.

| | A | B |
|---|---|---|
| | $000 | $000 |
| Revenue | 3,800 | 4,400 |
| Cost of sales | (2,700) | (2,820) |
| Gross profit | 1,100 | 1,580 |
| Distribution costs | (375) | (420) |
| Administrative expenses | (168) | (644) |
| Finance costs | (25) | (32) |
| Profit before tax | 532 | 484 |
| Income tax expense | (148) | (170) |
| PROFIT FOR THE YEAR | 384 | 314 |

**Extracts from statement of financial position**

| | $000 | $000 |
|---|---|---|
| Total equity | 950 | 1,500 |
| Non-current liabilities (borrowings) | 500 | 650 |
| Non-current assets | 1,700 | 1,500 |

## Additional information

■ A's administrative expenses include a gain of $350,000 on the disposal of non-current assets, following a major restructuring of the entity. The refocusing of the business activities also resulted in some capital investment which was undertaken near the end of its financial period.

■ A has a Held for Trading investment on the statement of financial position. Entity A made a gain on this investment of $20,000 in the period and this has been deducted from finance costs.

### Required:

(a) Prepare a report for presentation to the board of XYZ, which analyses the financial information provided and recommends the most suitable takeover target. (8 marks are available for the calculation of ratios). **(18 marks)**

(b) Explain the limitations of analysis when comparing two entities, using A and B as examples. **(7 marks)**

**(25 marks)**

# 4 Question four

## CIMA – Financial Analysis – November 2008

You are assistant to the Chief Financial Officer (CFO) of SWW, a large fashion retailer. SWW's merchandise is sourced from many different suppliers around the world. SWW's senior management has a business policy of building lasting relationships with suppliers either by investing in their shares, or by making loans to them at favourable rates of interest.

A request has recently been received from a supplier, TEX, for a loan of $25 million to allow it to invest in up to date machinery. The directors of TEX claim that the investment will result in efficiency improvements which, in the short to medium term, will allow it to reduce prices to its customers. SWW is a major customer of TEX, buying approximately 10% of TEX's annual output of cotton clothing.

In support of the application, TEX's CFO has supplied a one page report on the state of the business, and a statement of financial position and income statement for the year ended 30 September 2008. The 2008 figures are unaudited. TEX has not paid a dividend in the last five years. TEX's shares are listed on a local stock exchange, although the entity's founding family has retained a minor holding. TEX's functional and presentation currency is the $, and its financial statements are prepared in accordance with IFRS.

The financial statements supplied by TEX are as follows:

**TEX: consolidated income statement for the year ended 30 September 2008**

|  | 2008 | 2007 |
|---|---|---|
|  | $ million | $ million |
| Revenue | 256.3 | 281.7 |
| Cost of sales | (226.6) | (243.1) |
| Gross profit | 29.7 | 38.6 |
| Selling and distribution costs | (9.2) | (8.9) |
| Administrative expenses | (18.7) | (15.6) |
| Finance costs | (5.4) | (6.2) |
| Share of losses of associate | (1.3) | (6.8) |
| (Loss)/profit before tax | (4.9) | 1.1 |
| Income tax repayment (expense) | 1.5 | (0.4) |
| (Loss)/profit for the period | (3.4) | 0.7 |
| Attributable to: |  |  |
| Equity holders of parent | (3.2) | 0.6 |
| Minority interest | (0.2) | 0.1 |
|  | (3.4) | 0.7 |

# TEX: consolidated statement of financial position at 30 September 2008

|  | 2008 $ million | 2008 $ million | 2007 $ million | 2007 $ million |
|---|---|---|---|---|
| **ASSETS** | | | | |
| **Non-current assets:** | | | | |
| Property, plant and equipment | | 221.4 | | 227.3 |
| Investment in associate | | 13.8 | | 15.1 |
| Available for sale investments | | 2.6 | | 4.8 |
| | | 237.8 | | 247.2 |
| **Current assets:** | | | | |
| Inventories | 132.4 | | 125.6 | |
| Trade and other receivables | 51.7 | | 58.2 | |
| Cash | – | | 4.8 | |
| | | 184.1 | | 188.6 |
| | | 421.9 | | 435.8 |
| **EQUITY AND LIABILITIES** | | | | |
| **Equity** | | | | |
| Share capital ($1 shares) | 25.0 | | 25.0 | |
| Retained earnings and other reserves | 103.2 | | 106.2 | |
| Minority interest | 13.7 | | 13.9 | |
| | | 141.9 | | 145.1 |
| **Non-current liabilities:** | | | | |
| Long-term borrowings | 57.2 | | 67.1 | |
| Deferred tax | 18.0 | | 25.8 | |
| Defined benefit obligation | 26.0 | | 24.2 | |
| | | 101.2 | | 117.1 |
| Current liabilities: | | | | |
| Trade and other payables | 150.1 | | 161.2 | |
| Borrowings | 28.7 | | 12.4 | |
| | | 178.8 | | 173.6 |
| | | 421.9 | | 435.8 |

**Required:**

Produce a report to the CFO of SWW that:

(a) analyses and interprets the information given above from the point of view of SWW as a potential lender; **(20 marks)**

(b) describes the areas of uncertainty in the analysis and the nature of any additional information that will be required before a lending decision can be made. **(5 marks)**

Note: Up to 8 marks are available in part (a) for the calculation of relevant accounting ratios. **(25 marks)**

# 5 Question five

## CIMA – Financial Analysis – May 2009

ELB is an entity that manufactures and sells paper and packaging. For the last two years, the directors have pursued an aggressive policy of expansion. They have developed several new products and market share has increased.

ELB is finalising its financial statements for the year ended 31 December 2008. These will be presented to the Board of Directors at its next meeting, where the results for the year will be reviewed.

The statement of financial position at the year-end and its comparative for last year are presented below:

| | 2008 | | 2007 | |
|---|---|---|---|---|
| | $000 | $000 | $000 | $000 |
| **Assets** | | | | |
| **Non-current assets** | | | | |
| Property, plant and equipment | 25,930 | | 17,880 | |
| Investments available for sale | 6,200 | | 5,400 | |
| | | 32,130 | | 23,280 |
| **Current assets** | | | | |
| Inventories | 4,500 | | 3,600 | |
| Trade receivables | 4,300 | | 5,200 | |
| Cash and cash equivalents | - | | 120 | |
| | | 8,800 | | 8,920 |
| Total assets | | 40,930 | | 32,200 |
| **Equity and liabilities** | | | | |
| **Equity** | | | | |
| Share capital ($1 ordinary shares) | 10,000 | | 10,000 | |
| Revaluation reserve (Note 1) | 4,200 | | 1,100 | |
| Other reserves (Note 2) | 1,800 | | 1,000 | |
| Retained earnings | 7,460 | | 4,200 | |
| | | 23,460 | | 16,300 |
| **Non-current liabilities** | | | | |
| Term loan | 6,000 | | 6,000 | |
| 6% bonds 2010 (Note 3) | 5,400 | | 5,200 | |
| | | 11,400 | | 11,200 |
| **Current liabilities** | | | | |
| Trade and other payables | 5,800 | | 4,700 | |
| Short term borrowings | 270 | | - | |
| | | 6,070 | | 4,700 |
| Total equity and liabilities | | 40,930 | | 32,200 |

## Income statement for the year ended 31 December:

| | 2008 | 2007 |
|---|---|---|
| | $000 | $000 |
| Revenue | 34,200 | 28,900 |
| Cost of sales | (24,000) | (20,250) |
| Gross profit | 10,200 | 8,650 |
| Distribution costs and administrative expenses | (5,120) | (3,300) |
| Finance costs | (520) | (450) |
| Profit before tax | 4,560 | 4,900 |
| Income tax expense | (1,300) | (1,400) |
| Profit for the year | 3,260 | 3,500 |

**Note 1**

The movement on the revaluation reserve relates to property, plant and equipment that was revalued in the year.

**Note 2**

The movement on other reserves relates to the gains made on the available for sale investments.

**Note 3**

The bonds are repayable on 1 July 2010.

As part of their review, the directors will discuss certain key ratios that form part of the banking covenants in respect of the borrowing facilities as well as reviewing the performance in the year. The key ratios for the covenants include:

■ Gearing (debt/equity) target is 50%

■ Interest cover target is 9·5 times

■ Current ratio target is 1·5 : 1

■ Quick ratio target is 1·1 : 1

You are the assistant to the Chief Financial Officer of ELB and you have been asked to perform a preliminary review of, and prepare a commentary on, the year end figures. These comments will form part of the financial presentation to the board.

**Required:**

(a) Calculate the ratios required as part of the review of covenants and any other ratios that are relevant to assess the financial performance and position of ELB.

**(8 marks)**

(b) Prepare a report that explains the financial performance and position of ELB for presentation to the Board of Directors, including reference to the banking covenants.

**(12 marks)**

(c) Identify, and briefly describe, any other points that should be added to the meeting agenda for the Board of Directors to discuss in respect of the future financing of ELB.

**(5 marks)**

**(25 marks)**

# 6 Question six

## CIMA – Financial Analysis – November 2009

RG, a listed entity, invested significantly in one of its many operating segments in 2008, by acquiring property, plant and equipment and developing a new distribution network in an attempt to increase market share. The network has been put in place (distribution costs have been incurred within the set budget) and a new sales team has been hired and has just recently completed its product training. The first orders from the new customers were received in June 2009 and were higher than expected.

Extracts from the financial statements for RG for the year ended 30 June 2009 are presented below.

**Income statement for the year ended 30 June 2009 for the RG group**

|  | 2009 $m | 2008 $m |
|---|---|---|
| Revenue | 576 | 573 |
| Cost of sales | (422) | (428) |
| Gross profit | 154 | 145 |
| Distribution costs | (56) | (40) |
| Administrative expenses (including profit on disposal of investments) | (37) | (22) |
| Finance costs | (6) | (8) |
| Share of profit of associate | 5 | - |
| Profit before tax | 60 | 75 |
| Income tax expense | (15) | (14) |
| Profit for the period | 45 | 61 |
| Attributable to: |  |  |
| Equity holders of the parent | 37 | 52 |
| Minority interest | 8 | 9 |

## Statement of changes in equity

| | Share capital $m | Share premium $m | Other reserves $m | Retained earnings $m | Minority interest $m | Total $m |
|---|---|---|---|---|---|---|
| 1 July 2008 | 80 | 4 | 8 | 372 | 11 | 475 |
| Available for sale investments: | | | | | | |
| - gains to equity | | | 6 | | | 6 |
| - transfer on disposal | | | (4) | | | (4) |
| Profit for the period | | | | 37 | 8 | 45 |
| Dividends | | | | (50) | (5) | (55) |
| Issue of share capital | 30 | 18 | | | | 48 |
| 30 June 2009 | 110 | 22 | 10 | 359 | 14 | 515 |

## Statement of financial position as at 30 June 2009

|  | 2009 $m | 2008 $m |
|---|---|---|
| ASSETS | | |
| **Non-current assets** | | |
| Property, plant and equipment | 371 | 346 |
| Investment in associate | 85 | - |
| Available for sale investments | 65 | 140 |
| | 521 | 486 |
| **Current assets** | | |
| Inventories | 133 | 82 |
| Receivables | 109 | 76 |
| Cash and cash equivalents | 12 | 137 |
| | 254 | 295 |
| **Total assets** | 775 | 781 |
| EQUITY AND LIABILITIES | | |
| **Attributable to the equity shareholders of the parent:** | | |
| Called up share capital ($1 shares) | 110 | 80 |
| Share premium | 22 | 4 |
| Other reserves | 10 | 8 |
| Retained earnings | 359 | 372 |
| | 501 | 464 |
| Minority interest | 14 | 11 |
| **Total equity** | 515 | 475 |
| Non-current liabilities | | |
| Long term loan | 154 | 205 |
| Current liabilities | | |
| Trade payables | 91 | 87 |
| Income tax payable | 15 | 14 |
| | 106 | 101 |
| Total equity and liabilities | 775 | 781 |

A close friend of yours has inherited a portfolio of investments which includes a holding in RG. He is contemplating whether to retain or sell his shareholding. As he does not have a financial background he is looking for your advice. In his email to you he appeared to be focusing his initial conclusions on the decreased profitability of the business but wanted your opinion on the profitability and financial health of RG. He also wants your thoughts on its future prospects. He mentioned that he had had a quick look at the segmental information provided in the financial statements but was confused by the volume of numerical information and was questioning whether a review of the segmental information was relevant for his purposes. To help with your review he has sent through extracts from the financial statements, shown above, but has not provided any segmental information.

Required:

(a) Prepare a report that analyses the financial performance and position of RG to assist your friend in his decision making. (8 marks are available for the calculation of relevant ratios.) **(21 marks)**

(b) Briefly discuss how useful segmental analysis could be in the analysis of RG's financial statements. **(4 marks)**

**(25 marks)**

# 7 Question seven

## CIMA – Financial Analysis – November 2009

BCA is a multinational entity and part of its business is the operation of power stations. Minimising pollution is of primary concern to the entity and therefore it has contracts with CAD, a relatively new and innovative entity, to undertake regular monitoring of the output of potentially hazardous gases from the stations.

CAD utilises sophisticated equipment that is highly sensitive to many gases. The equipment and related software were developed by CAD using innovative techniques created by the Chief Scientific Officer (CSO) who has extensive expertise in gas sensing and laser physics. A number of CAD's products have been patented. As the CSO is considered to be a vital part of the entity's ongoing success, CAD required her to sign a nine month contract. This contract prevents her from developing similar products for anyone else for a further 12 months. The CSO was also given a bonus this year, as the development of new technology helped to secure a lucrative four year contract with a new customer. It is likely to bring additional revenues from existing contracts over the next couple of years. The CSO has an equity stake in the business as does the Chief Executive.

Despite having another three key contracts, similar to the one with BCA, CAD is struggling financially and is desperately in need of investment. CAD is having difficulty raising finance as it has very few tangible assets on which security can be offered.

The directors of CAD have approached the board of BCA to ask for investment and have indicated that they would be willing to give up their controlling interest in CAD if the entity's future and their own, could be secured.

## Summary financial information is provided below:

| Income statement for the year ended 30 September 2009 for CAD | 2009 | 2008 |
|---|---|---|
| | $000 | $000 |
| Revenue | 4,330 | 3,562 |
| Cost of sales | (3,702) | (2,810) |
| Gross profit | 628 | 752 |
| Other operating expenses | (465) | (580) |
| Finance costs | (13) | (2) |
| Profit before tax | 150 | 170 |
| Income tax expense | (42) | (45) |
| Profit for the period | 108 | 125 |

| Statement of financial position as at 30 September 2009 for CAD | 2009 | 2008 |
|---|---|---|
| | $000 | $000 |
| ASSETS | | |
| **Non-current assets** | | |
| Property, plant and equipment | 52 | 78 |
| Intangible assets | 89 | 38 |
| | 141 | 116 |
| **Current assets** | | |
| Inventories | 125 | 72 |
| Trade receivables | 1,091 | 587 |
| Cash and cash equivalents | 58 | 318 |
| | 1,274 | 977 |
| **Total assets** | 1,415 | 1,093 |
| EQUITY AND LIABILITIES | | |
| **Equity attributable to equity owners of the parent** | | |
| Share capital ($1 ordinary shares) | 4 | 4 |
| Retained earnings | 539 | 431 |
| **Total equity** | 543 | 435 |
| **Non-current liabilities** | | |
| Provisions | 62 | 173 |
| **Current liabilities** | | |
| Trade and other payables | 687 | 485 |
| Short term borrowings | 123 | - |
| Total current liabilities | 810 | 485 |
| Total Liabilities | 872 | 658 |
| Total equity and liabilities | 1,415 | 1,093 |

**Required:**

(a) Prepare a preliminary report for the board of BCA, highlighting the key considerations of CAD as a potential target for acquisition. Your report should include discussion of the key challenges that CAD faces and whether these would change if BCA were to acquire CAD. (5 marks are available for relevant ratios that can aid your discussion.) **(15 marks)**

(b)(i) Explain why there is increasing pressure to extend the scope of corporate reporting and why this may result in an increase in narrative reporting. **(4 marks)**

(ii) Discuss why a report, similar to the UK's Operating and Financial Review, might be helpful to potential investors in CAD. **(6 marks)**

**(25 marks)**

# Suggested solutions

## 1 Question one

### 1. Check the exact requirements

We are asked to explain the usefulness of related party disclosures (not just set out the requirements in IAS 24) and analyse the financial statements of Mossylea in a form suggested by our Managing Director. This means that the analysis should be structured in the required format.

### 2. Read the whole question and note significant information

■ Mossylea is owned by Fructose, who wishes to sell. A significant proportion of Mossylea's revenue comes from sales to Fructose. This may not continue following a sale of Mossylea.

■ Raw material prices are rising faster than selling prices. This is likely to have an adverse impact on future profitability.

■ Fructose provides management services to Mossylea. It is unclear whether these are given free of charge, or charged at an arms length rate.

■ There is general upward pressure on costs and new revenue lines have not proved popular.

■ A significant investment in non-current assets was made in late 2007. This would potentially cause ratios like ROCE to be depleted in 2007, because the investment would not have contributed increased profits for the whole of 2007 but would be reflected in the capital employed number.

■ The tax charge for the current period is very unrepresentative due to the adverse effect of a tax investigation that was settled in the current year.

→

### 3. Review the financial statements and note the key trends arising

■ There has been a healthy increase in revenues and gross profit. However £0.7 million of the overall revenue increase of £0.873 million has arisen due to increases in sales to Fructose.

■ The halving of the management charge has contributed to the significant growth in operating profit.

■ The increase in operating margins, although impressive, still leaves Mossylea below the industry average.

■ The finance cost of the loan from Fructose is 2%. This is almost certainly below market rates.

■ A significant amount of total funding is provided by Fructose. This would presumably need to be replaced should the acquisition go ahead.

■ The net assets of Mossylea have not changed significantly and short term liquidity looks satisfactory.

■ It is notable that retained earnings are negative. This need not mean, though, that Mossylea does not have a bright future.

### 4. Calculation of pre-determined ratios

These are not required in this question.

### 5. Selective calculation of additional ratios

This is done in the appendix to the actual answer. The supplied ratios do not include ones that relate to liquidity and solvency so calculations of this type would be useful.

### 6. Overall conclusions

■ The rise in ROCE appears to reflect a profitability improvement.

■ It is important to evaluate the impact of trading with Fructose on the overall results.

- Given the investment in non-current assets towards the end of 2007 it is surprising that asset turnover and non-current asset turnover are relatively unchanged.

- A key factor driving the rise in ROCE is the improved operating margin (the gross margin is largely unchanged) and this is affected by the halving of the management charge from Fructose.

- The underlying efficiency ratios are satisfactory.

- As an overall conclusion it would appear at least possible that the results of Mossylea are affected by its relationship with Fructose and this should be taken into account when making any decision regarding a possible future purchase of Mossylea.

**Answer in report format.**

**(a)** Related party relationships are common in business and commerce. In group situations where one entity exercises control over another, the holding company can direct the financial and operating policy of the subsidiary for the benefit of the group rather than any individual company. Related party transactions affect the profit or loss and the financial position of entities. Transactions may be undertaken that would not normally have occurred if the business were independent. In addition the terms of those transactions (such as prices, payment periods) may not be the same as if they had been between unrelated parties.

The financial performance and financial position may be affected by the related party relationship even if transactions do not occur. Where one party has control over the other they may direct their activities in a number of ways such as spending on advertising.

Related party disclosures help users make assessments about financial statements including the risk and opportunities facing organisations.

**(b)** Further ratios could be calculated. For example:

|  | 2008 | 2007 |
|---|---|---|
| NB: Capital employed | 980 + 2,500 − 70 = **3,410** | 660 + 2,500 − 50 = **3,110** |
| **Performance and efficiency ratios** | | |
| Gross margin % | 21.9% | 22.1% |
| Operating margin % – excluding. management charge | 13.4% | 13.0% |
| Operating expenses % | 8.5% | 9.1% |
| Non-current asset turnover (Revenue/Non-current assets) | 2.63 times | 2.59 times |
| Net asset turnover (Revenue/ Capital Employed) | 2.85 times | 2.86 times |
| **Financial position and liquidity ratios** | | |
| Gearing (Debt:equity) | 248% | 371% |
| Current ratio | 0.88 | 0.86 |
| Trade receivables collection period | 42 days | 47 days |
| Trade payables payment period | 88 days | 100 days |
| Inventory turnover | 15.5 times | 15.1 times |
| Interest cover | 16.0 times | 3.2 times |

## Introduction

A first look at the information indicates that net profit has improved considerably year on year. This is particularly impressive considering the significant cost pressures which more than offset the increase in selling prices.

A review of the statement of financial position highlights that PPE is the most significant asset and a significant investment was made in late 2007. This may have been financed by Fructose which has a significant loan outstanding to Mossylea.

The notes to the financial statements indicate that transactions with related parties may have a significant impact on the financial statements. The note does not indicate that they are at arms length. Per IAS 24, Related Party Disclosures, this does not mean that they are not but means that Mossylea's management either cannot substantiate the fact or chose not to.

## Profitability

The return on capital employed (ROCE) has increased from 5.1% to 23.5% giving the indication that the overall efficiency of management in employing the resources of the group has improved. This is primarily due to the four-fold increase in profit from operations, which in turn is significantly affected by the halving of the management charge from Fructose.

Revenue has grown by 9.3% year on year. This is in part due to selling prices having increased by 7% but also sales volumes must have increased. Bread is a staple product and sales volumes should be resilient to increasing prices. However, the major impact on revenue growth appears to be the increase in revenue derived from sales to Fructose.

Taking this into consideration, revenue to third parties has grown from £8.6 million (8,900 less 300) to £8.73 million (9,730 less 1,000) which represents only 1.5%. This is significantly less than sales price increases of 7% and suggests that sales volumes to third parties have probably decreased. This is consistent with the statement that an additional range of products had proved unpopular.

Gross margins have reduced marginally by 0.2 percentage points. Given the significant cost increases in third party raw material input prices and the increases in energy costs, a more marked fall would have been more likely. It could be that favourable margins have been obtained on sales to Fructose which has more than offset the decrease in margins on sales to third parties.

Operating expenses (excluding the management charge) have not increased significantly year on year and probably reflect general inflationary pressures.

The management charge has reduced by 50%. An explanation of what is included in the charge, whether it is reasonable and the likely cost of replacing those services with third party services should be sought.

The operating margin has increased significantly. With gross margins broadly stable and operating expenses remaining fairly static this appears to be largely as a result of the reduction in the management charge. However, the operating margin is still significantly below the industry average. If the management charge is excluded the adjusted operating margin is 13.4% (2007 – 13.1%). This is more comparable year on year.

Interest cover has increased approximately in line with the profitability increase. The interest expense represents a fixed rate of interest on funds borrowed from Fructose. At 2% it is obviously not on an arms length basis and is below commercial lending rates. Orrell would probably need to replace it with borrowings with a higher rate of interest following an acquisition.

Non-current asset and net asset turnover have remained very similar year on year. This is somewhat surprising given the significant level of capital expenditure in 2007. This expenditure does not appear to have delivered any apparent benefits. The ratio of capital expenditure to depreciation demonstrates that investment may be simply replacing worn out assets.

The evidence may suggest that the financial performance of Mossylea has been manipulated with a view to selling the company. Related party transactions such as increasing revenues and reducing costs have benefited performance. In addition, new product ventures appear to have failed. The underlying profitability is not clear.

### Financial position (inc. liquidity and solvency)

Gearing is significant at 248%. It has fallen since the prior year. However, the indebtedness is to the parent company. Upon acquisition it is likely that Fructose would want the amount repaying.

The current ratio is almost unchanged at 0.88 times. This may at first appear low but given that cash flows include related party trading transactions, the working capital cycle is not simple to understand. For example, the trade receivable collection period has fallen by 5 days but this could be significantly affected by Fructose paying for goods on receipt or with only a short credit period.

The trade payable payment period has reduced. The terms for major suppliers need investigating to establish the reasons behind that.

Inventory turnover has improved marginally. In the food industry it would be expected to be high given the nature of the product.

The debit balance on retained earnings indicates that Mossylea is unlikely to be in a position to pay dividends until it is cleared.

**Further matters for investigation (see above also)**

■ More detail on the term and conditions of trading transactions with Fructose. In particular whether selling prices are at arms length and whether these transactions are likely to continue following a change in ownership, such as if contracts are in place.

■ Whether the management charge represents identifiable and measurable services provided. Would Orrell incur the same expenditure in providing equivalent services?

■ The reason for the 50% year on year reduction in the management charge.

■ Details of any services received from Fructose for which no fees have been paid.

■ Details of the major capital expenditure in 2007 and the benefits derived from it.

■ Details of future capital expenditure plans and asset replacement policies.

■ Industry (sector specific) comparisons for the industry ratios (such as gross margins) to ascertain performance against the sector.

■ How the debit balance on retained earnings arose and the availability of distributable reserves.

■ The nature and reasons behind the additional tax payment of £200,000 and whether any issues remain outstanding.

■ Trade receivables collection period for transactions with third parties to assess the terms of trade.

# Suggested solutions

## 2 Question two

### 1. Checking of exact requirements

There are two requirements here. The first asks us to comment on the benefits and limitations of segment reporting. We must be careful with a requirement like this not just to reproduce the requirements of the relevant standard, in this case IFRS8. We should rather evaluate the usefulness of the standard. The second asks us to evaluate the financial performance and financial position of a group where the yardstick of comparison is the previous period.

### 2. Reading of all the information that is given and consideration of the potential implications for financial analysis

■ Trindac has acquired a new subsidiary in the current period. The takeover was hostile and the previous directors have set up a rival organisation that could be a potential threat to revenues.

■ There appears to be a necessity to pay dividends each year to satisfy the aspirations of the founder shareholders.

■ The availability of segment information would make it sensible to compute some ratios on a segmental basis to ascertain the relative contributions of the different segments to the overall performance of the group.

■ There has been a very large purchase of goodwill on acquisition of Ensmarr (nearly £30m). This is apparently due to the existence of a highly skilled workforce. Unless there are medium term service contracts in place this could become impaired quite quickly.

→

3. Reviewing the financial statements as a whole and considering what the major differences are between the financial statements for the two periods

■ There has been significant revenue growth (to be expected given the acquisition of Ensmarr) but very little growth in gross profit or operating profit.

■ The additional finance costs caused by borrowings taken out to finance the acquisition has resulted in a fall in pre-tax profits.

■ There has been a greater percentage increase in operating cash flow than the percentage increase in operating profit. This could well be caused by the impact of the acquisition on the 'cash flow cycle'.

■ The new acquisition has introduced an income stream that seems to be more profitable than the existing stream. This has only had a nine month impact in 2008. In 2009 and future years the impact will be for a full period and therefore more marked.

■ A 'downside' of the acquisition is the increase in gearing.

## 4. Calculating up to five additional ratios

There are a number of additional ratios that could potentially be useful for the analysis but the ones that will add the most value are likely to be the 'profitability' ratios, both overall and on a segment basis.

### (i) Return on capital employed (ROCE)

| | 2008 | 2007 |
|---|---|---|
| Book value of equity (£'000) | 152.5 | 130.9 |
| Net debt (£'000) | 197.8 | 122.6 |
| So total capital employed | 350.3 | 253.5 |
| Profit from operations (£'000) | 21.4 | 20.2 |
| So ROCE | 21.4/350.3 = **6.1%** | 20.2/253.5 = **8.0%** |

### (ii) Gross profit margin

| | 2008 | 2007 |
|---|---|---|
| Gross profit (£'000) | 26.5 | 24.0 |
| Revenue (£'000) | 230.5 | 193 |
| So gross margin | 26.5/230.5 = **11.5%** | 24/193 = **12.4%** |

### (iii) Operating profit margin

| | 2008 | 2007 |
|---|---|---|
| Profit from operations (£'000) | 21.4 | 20.2 |
| Revenue (£'000) | 230.5 | 193 |
| So operating margin | 21.4/230.5 = **9.3%** | 20.2/193 = **10.5%** |

### (iv) Gross margin by segment for 2008

|  | General waste | Specialist waste |
|---|---|---|
| Gross profit (£'000) | 20.3 | 6.2 |
| Revenue (£'000) | 191.5 | 39 |
| So gross margin | 20.3/191.5 = **10.6%** | 6.2/39 = **15.9%** |

### (v) Operating margin by segment

|  | General waste | Specialist waste |
|---|---|---|
| Profit from operations (£'000) | 16.2 | 5.2 |
| Revenue (£'000) | 191.5 | 39 |
| So gross margin | 16.2/191.5 = **8.4%** | 5.2/39 = **13.3%** |

## 5. Analysis of ratios provided and computed

- There is a trend of declining profitability, both in the existing and in the acquired business. This could partly be due to the costs of integrating the two business, particularly in the case of the newly acquired business.

- Non-current asset turnover has declined. This could be at least partly due to the inclusion of a large amount of goodwill in non-current assets.

- There has been a significant increase in gearing, as the acquisition was basically financed by borrowings. This will affect the risk profile of the group. This may have been responsible for the decline in the PE ratio since last year.

- The dividend has been cut, possibly because of the strain on cash caused by the acquisition.

- Although the group has suffered a cash outflow, the generation of cash from operating activities may well, if repeated in future years, mean there is no long term liquidity issue.

## 6. Suggested answer

### Part (a)

### Benefits of IFRS 8 segment information:

It is potentially very useful for all classes of financial statement user to have access to disaggregated information. Highly aggregated information can mask important underlying trends in significant parts of the business, making it very difficult for users to undertake meaningful analysis.

The approach that IFRS 8 takes to the identification of segments allows users some access to the type of information that is available to the chief operating decision maker in the business; it allows them to see 'through the eyes of management'.

### Limitations of IFRS 8 segment information:

The level of disclosure of segment information, and the definition of segments, is at the discretion of management. Managers may be reluctant, for perfectly sound commercial reasons, to make extensive disclosures, and so users' access to information is always less than they would, ideally, like.

The definition of segments depends upon the way in which segments are identified and managed within the business. Even businesses that are engaged in apparently similar activities may organise their businesses in very different ways. Therefore the extent of true comparability between businesses is always likely to be limited.

Given the typical level of segment information disclosure, it is not possible for users to calculate a range of important key ratios. For example, there is no requirement in IFRS 8 to allocate share capital and borrowings to segments, so in the absence of additional, voluntary, disclosures, it is not possible to calculate segment return on capital employed. There is no requirement for the presented items to be measured in accordance with IFRS; the requirement is that they are measured as presented to the chief operating decision maker. The consequence is that users of the financial statements could be confused or even misled.

Comparability between entities is compromised by the fact that IFRS 8 does not provide definitions of some key accounting elements: for example, the standard does not define 'segment profit or loss' or 'segment assets'.

## Part (b)

Up to 5 marks are available for the calculation of additional ratios. These have already been computed.

**Report**
To: Gloria
From: Adviser

### Analysis of extracts from Trindac plc's financial statements for the 2008 financial year

### Introduction

Trindac plc has experienced a significant change in its activities during the 2008 financial year with the acquisition of a controlling stake in Ensmarr which was intended to help to reverse the trend of Trindac's declining profitability. The first set of financial statements from the enlarged group suggest, however, that the trend has not been reversed.

The acquisition was financed through an increase in borrowings, thus increasing ordinary shareholders' exposure to risk. To date, it appears that they have not gained a commensurate increase in return.

### Performance

The consolidated figures show a decrease in profitability, in both gross margin and operating margin. Examination of the disaggregated figures provided in the segment disclosures shows that the decline is across both segments. There is an apparent downward trend in the general waste management business, comparing the segment information with last year's totals, which accounts for over 80% of the group's revenue and which has produced a fall in gross margin from 12.4% to 10.6%.

There has also been a fairly significant fall in gross profitability in the specialist waste business. Under its original management the business produced a gross margin of 17.2% but this has fallen to just 15.9% under Trindac's management. However, this may not be a permanent fall; there was almost certainly some disruption to operations around the time of the acquisition which would adversely affect margins. It would be helpful to know whether or not margins had recovered towards the end of the year, but this information is not likely to be readily accessible.

The analysis of operating margins reveals similar effects to those observed in the gross margin analysis, although the effect at operating margin level is even more pronounced in Ensmarr. There is a full 2 percentage point fall in operating margin under the new management, suggesting some difficulty in controlling costs.

A key point of interest for you and other shareholders is the level of dividend received. Although overall profitability of the Trindac business had decreased only slightly, dividends were cut by one third in 2008. Given the level of profits it would appear that, all other things being equal, Trindac could have maintained the dividend at its 2007 level.

The group's PE ratio tends to suggest that the market has lost some confidence in the business, and the cut in dividend may have contributed to this effect. However, it is worth pointing out that the dramatic drop in share price between June 2007 and June 2008 (a decrease of 63.5%) may have more to do with macro-economic trends and the general fall in share values that has taken place over the period. It would be worth finding out whether the fall in Trindac's share price has been greater or lesser than the average experienced in its sector.

**Financial position**

Trindac's directors may have decided to cut the dividend because of concerns about cash flow and the group's gearing level. The financial position information provided shows that gearing has increased by a large, and worrying, margin. It appears, from the cash flow information, that the acquisition of the shares in Ensmarr was funded principally, if not wholly, by an increase in borrowings. It may be significant that

Trindac's directors did not choose to ask shareholders for additional equity investment, for example, in the form of a rights issue; it may indicate that shareholders would have been reluctant to commit further funds to the business. However, the substantial increase in borrowings has significantly increased the risk to which the group and the shareholders are exposed. Interest cover is poor at only 1.56, significantly less than in 2007.

## Cash flow

Some reassuring aspects of the cash flow analysis have been mentioned already, and in addition, cash from operations as a percentage of profit from operations is apparently healthy at 325% (2007: 259%). However, while the ratios are satisfactory in respect of cash generated from operations, the whole picture presented by the statement of cash flows is less reassuring. The substantial purchase of the controlling interest in Ensmarr is almost matched by significant investment in property, plant and equipment, which accounts for virtually the whole amount of cash generated by operations. There is insufficient information available to take this part of the analysis further (see below), but it is worth noting that the non-current asset turnover ratio has diminished significantly between the two years. It could be that the bulk of the investment in property, plant and equipment took place towards the end of the year, and that there has not been sufficient time available to generate revenue from it. It may also be the case that the Ensmarr ratio is particularly low, and that this has depressed the overall group ratio.

## Working capital

There has been a significant worsening of some of the working capital ratios. The current ratio, at significantly less than 1 is potentially a cause for concern, as is the fact that the group is taking around 3 months on average to meet its current trade payables. Although the information is not given, it is likely that the group is suffering from a shortage of ready cash. This is a factor that may have influenced the directors' decision to cut the dividend.

### Key points arising from the analysis

The trend of the ratios suggests that Trindac may be struggling to absorb the operations of Ensmarr. However, it is possible that the worst of the struggle is over, and that the combined businesses are by now working well. It is not possible to conclude on this point without a great deal of extra information.

It is worrying that the directors resigned from Ensmarr immediately following takeover. They had apparently been very successful in running a specialist waste business, and it is possible that the higher margins they achieved prior to takeover cannot now be maintained under the Trindac management. It is also a matter of concern that they immediately set up a competitor business. Their combined expertise, contacts in the business and experience of negotiating contracts with hospitals may make them a formidable competitor. It is possible that the ex-directors were able to persuade some of Ensmarr's customers to transfer to their new business.

The level of risk to the ordinary shareholders of the group has been significantly increased with the very large increase in debt capital. To date, they have not seen any commensurate return, and have even suffered a drop in dividend. At current levels of gearing, Trindac may find it very difficult to borrow much more cash, so if cash is required for new projects it may be more likely that the directors will appeal to shareholders for it.

A significant proportion of the price paid for Ensmarr was

in respect of goodwill. The managing director's comments suggest that the group acquired the benefits of Ensmarr's reputation and workforce. (Neither of these attributes could be recognised as intangible assets under IFRS). There is no sign from the information given that any impairment of this amount has been recognised in the 2008 financial statements, and so it must be assumed that its value has not diminished, even though the directors who were apparently responsible for the company's success left immediately. However, it is a substantial sum in the context of group profitability, and any impairment could have a significant effect in future on group profits. There might be some justifiable concern that the price paid for the investment proves over time to be excessive.

**Matters requiring further investigation** (see also points made earlier in the report)

Investigation of the activities of the previous Ensmarr directors subsequent to their resignation should be undertaken. If information is available about the competitor business they established it should be investigated. It is possible that they will be able to compete successfully for hospital waste contracts when they come up for renewal in future, and indeed, they may already have been successful in this.

The financial statements of Trindac for the 2008 financial year should be examined in detail to see if any impairment of the goodwill on acquisition of Ensmarr was recognised.

Information about non-current asset acquisitions, disposals and depreciation policy should be ascertained from the financial statements in order to establish whether the investment of £52.1 million comprises replacement of worn-out assets or new investments.

Industry sector comparisons could be useful to see if, for example, the current ratio is generally below 1.

# Suggested solutions

## 3  Question three

### 1. Checking of the exact requirements

The question asks for a comparative report that analyses the financial statements of two entities that are considered as possible takeover targets, and a discussion of the limitations of financial analysis (notice how often this requirement, or something similar, appears in these types of question).

### 2. Reading of all the information that is given and consideration of the potential implications for financial analysis

■ A and B are sufficiently similar to be validly comparable.

■ Profitability, efficiency and risk are key areas for analysis.

■ We appear to be directed to compute certain key ratios. A maximum of 8 marks is available for this so it would not be a wise use of time to compute many (if any) more.

■ A has made a one-off gain that needs to be allowed for when making any comparisons.

■ The sale of a 'held for trading' investment by A has also positively contributed to its profits in the current period.

■ A has made some capital investment towards the end of the most recent accounting period.

→

3. Reviewing the financial statements as a whole and considering what the major differences are between the financial statements of the two entities

- The revenue and gross profit of B is considerably higher than that of A.

- The above situation is reversed at profit before tax level but this is largely due to the two 'one-off' items in A (see 2 above).

- The effective tax rates are significantly different. However the question does tell us the two entities operate in different tax regimes.

- It is notable that A's non-current assets are larger than B's and yet B has greater sales revenues. This may be partly due to the investment made by A in non-current assets just before the year end.

## 4. Calculation of ratios

| | A | A | B | B |
|---|---|---|---|---|
| Gross profit margin :GP/sales | 1,100/3,800 | 29% | 1,580/4,400 | 36% |
| Profit margin : PBT/sales | 532/3,800 | 14% | 484/4,400 | 11% |
| Profit margin after adjustments | 532-350-20/3,800 | 4% | | |
| Gearing (debt/equity) | 500/950 | 53% | 650/1,500 | 43% |
| Non-current asset turnover | 3,800/1,700 | 2.24 | 4,400/1,500 | 2.93 |
| ROCE | (532 + 25)/1,450 | 38% | (484 + 32)/2,150 | 24% |
| ROCE after adjustment | 532+25-350-20/1,450 | 13% | | |
| Finance costs: interest/debt | 25/500 | 5% | 32/650 | 5% |
| Adjusted for investment gain | 45/500 | 9% | | |
| Distribution costs/sales | 375/3,800 | 10% | 420/4,400 | 10% |
| Administration expenses/sales | 168/3,800 | 4% | 644/4,400 | 15% |
| Adjusted for NCA gain | 518/3,800 | 14% | | |
| Tax rate: tax/PBT | 148/532 | 28% | 170/484 | 35% |

## 5. Analysis of ratios

■ At gross profit level the profit margin of B is superior to that of A.

■ The above trend is apparently reversed at net profit level but this reversal is entirely due to one-off gains arising for A during the period.

■ After allowing for the one-off gain on disposal of the AFS investment, the effective finance costs of A appear to be higher than those of B. This may not matter though in the context of a potential takeover as in such circumstances the acquired business if often re-financed.

■ The non-current asset turnover ratio shows that B appears to be utilising its assets more efficiently than A. However as stated above A has recently invested in new assets that will not have generated revenues for a full year, thus tending to reduce this ratio.

■ The gearing of A is considerably higher than that of B. However, as already stated, this may not matter too much if the acquired business is refinanced.

## Requirement (a)

**Report to: the Board of XYZ**
**Subject: potential acquisitions**

The gross profit margin of B, 36% is significantly higher than that of A, 29%, indicating that B has greater control over its core cost of sales. However A has managed to achieve 14% profit before tax compared with B's 11%. This would normally indicate that A has better control of administrative and distribution costs than B, however there have been two notable transactions that have had a significant impact on A's profit before tax.

1. A gain of $350,000 on the disposal of a non-current asset was offset against administrative expenses. Adjusting for this one-off gain increases administrative expenses by $350,000 and results in admin expenses of 14% of sales, which is line with B.

2. On the face of it both entities pay approximately 5% for finance (based on interest/long term borrowings). However A holds held for trading investments and has recorded gains of $20,000 in the year to finance costs. When this is removed the finance costs are $45,000, which means that A is paying around 9% for its borrowings. This indicates that A is considered by the lender(s) to be a riskier investment.

   The gearing ratio of A is 53% compared with B's gearing of 43%. B is likely to be viewed as a less risky investment by financiers if additional funding was required.

   B's gross margin is considerably higher than A's and yet only achieves a profit before tax percentage of 11%. This might be something that could be improved on acquisition if the combined entity could take advantage of economies of scale. Based on the reported figures A's profit before tax is

14% of sales but if the non-current asset gain is removed (assuming that this is a non-recurring item) then this profit falls to less than 5%, which is significantly less than B.

Furthermore, the efficiency level of B appears to be higher than A when we compare non-current asset turnover, A's being 2.24 and B's being 2.93. A, however, recently refocused business activities and invested in non-current assets. These assets may not yet be providing return which would deflate the NCA turnover ratio. Entity B may have older assets and be in need of investment. This may suit us as we can align any investment with our own business strategy.

The tax regimes may play a significant role in the decision on acquisition. A pays approximately 28% tax based on tax/profit before tax. B pays approximately 35% tax. This is something that should be investigated further before proceeding with either acquisition.

On the basis of this initial review, **I would recommend that entity B be considered further for acquisition, based on the profitability, efficiency and low risk indicated by the gearing and interest costs.**

## Requirement (b)

Although A and B operate in similar sectors, it is unlikely that any two entities will have the same operating environments and as a result will produce different results. Different activities and strategies will affect the comparability, e.g. A's decision to invest in held for trading investments which produce gains/losses.

The financial statements given are for one period only and are not necessarily covering the same 12 month period. The information provided may cover a period that is not typical of the trend of performance over a longer period of time and may be affected by non-recurring items, e.g. A's gain on the sale of non-current assets.

Despite the increasing levels of accounting guidance, entities still have considerable discretion in the way financial transactions are recorded. Adopting different accounting policies can affect comparability, e.g. equity of one entity could include revaluation of non-current assets and the other may hold non-current assets at depreciated historic cost. This would affect ratios such as return on capital employed and non-current asset turnover.

Before making an acquisition it is important to consider the non-financial factors. An entity's social and environmental policy may be in line with the acquirer's strategy and finding the best business fit may be as important as the financial information.

# Suggested solutions

## 4 │ Question four

### 1. Checking of exact requirements

We (SWW) are considering making a loan to an entity – 'Tex'. We
have received some unaudited financial information relating to Tex
and are required to evaluate it from a lending perspective, indicating
the possible limitations in our analysis.

### 2. Overview of all the information and consideration of the implications for the analysis

■ Tex wants a loan of $25 million to invest in plant and equipment.

■ Tex has paid no dividend for five years, possibly due to liquidity
problems?

■ SWW is a key customer of Tex. It's relatively unusual for a supplier
to ask a customer for a loan. Could this be because they have been
refused credit elsewhere? This is surprising for a listed entity.

### 3. Review of the financial statements as a whole

Revenues have fallen significantly leading to a loss-making situation.

■ Tex has a loss-making associate. Given that these statements are
unaudited we should raise the issue of possible impairment.

■ Inventories have risen even though sales have fallen. This could
indicate obsolescence problems given that the financial statements
are unaudited.

■ It is unclear without computing the relevant ratio what has
happened to receivables days. Trade receivables have fallen but
then so have sales.

■ There is a defined benefit pension liability in the statement of
financial position. It is unclear whether the costs have been
reflected in the income statement in accordance with IAS 19.

→

■ Short term borrowings have increased significantly since last year.

■ Trade payables are three times trade receivables! This is a most unusual occurrence and would seem to indicate possible difficulty in settling these amounts.

### 4. Calculation of ratios required by question

Not required here.

### 5. Calculation of additional ratios (8 marks maximum)

Where 8 marks are available this means 4-8 ratios as a maximum would be computed. Some key ones appear as an appendix to the report.

### 6. Analysis of ratios

Profitability is adversely affected by a significant fall in revenues that has impacted on both profit margins and asset turnover.

The real level of inventory has increased significantly which could be tied to the reduction in revenues and (given that we have unaudited financial statements) could indicate the presence of obsolete inventory.

Liquidity levels have worsened and gearing has increased.

All in all this loan request needs to be judged with caution. However it may be worthwhile if it secures future supplies for SWW. Further investigation would be needed.

**From: Accountant**

**To: CFO**

**Report on TEX loan application**

(a) TEX's performance has deteriorated significantly between 2007 and 2008. Revenue in 2008 has decreased by 9% on the previous year's figure, and the fall in gross profitability has been even more significant. Gross margin in 2007 was 13.7%, falling to only 11.6% in 2008, and the business is now loss-making. Asset turnover has decreased, which may suggest inefficiencies in operation, or possibly deteriorating performance from old machinery. Performance is not helped by the results of the associate whose loss, although not as large as in 2007, has contributed significantly to the overall loss. The statement of financial position valuation of the investment in associate has not, apparently, been reduced by the recognition of any impairment losses. If the investment is impaired, the impairment loss would further increase the loss for the year.

Turning to the statement of financial position, the position is worse in most respects than in 2007. The business is holding a very large amount of inventory, even more than in 2007, thus tying up cash and incurring holding costs. A significant proportion of inventory could be raw material and there may be good reasons why large amounts should be held at the end of September. However, it is also possible that some of the inventory is obsolete, and should be written off, which again would increase the loss for the year.

Receivables turnover is slow, but that could be expected in this business. It has actually improved slightly between 2007 and 2008, which may mean that management has made a definite effort to speed up cash collection.

By the end of September 2008 the business has no cash in hand, and its balance of available for sale investments which could, presumably, be realised in an emergency, is almost halved from the previous year end. Borrowings net of cash at the 2007 year end were $74.7 million ($67.1 + 12.4 − 4.8), but by the end of 2008 they had increased to $85.9 ($57.2 + 28.7), and gearing had increased substantially. The large increase in borrowings is a worrying sign, but so also is the fact that a much higher proportion of the total is classified in current liabilities. On the face of it, the business will have difficulty meeting its current liabilities as they fall due, an impression which is reinforced by the very low quick ratio. Trade and other payables have fallen, but the total of $150.1 million outstanding at the end of 2008 is extremely high in the context of the other statement of financial position figures. It is likely that many of TEX's suppliers are not in a position to complain about non-payment of amounts owing, but there is the danger that it could force some of its suppliers out of business.

The level of interest cover is not attractive to a potential lender. It is surprising to note that interest has actually fallen in 2008 compared to 2007. This may mean that at other times of year the position is not as bad as it appears at the year end. Nevertheless, the position is so poor as to provide a significant deterrent to SWW as a potential lender. There are additional sources of concern in the other long-term liabilities. The net liability on the pension scheme is significant in size at both year ends, and it may indicate on-going difficulties in funding the obligations under the scheme. The deferred tax balance is also significant and is a prospective, if not immediate, cause for concern.

If the position and performance of TEX continues to deteriorate in line with current trends, it is quite possible that the business will become insolvent in the foreseeable future.

On the evidence provided so far, a loan to TEX would be very risky, and there would be a significant probability of non-recovery.

**November 2008**

(b) The analysis above is subject to a great deal of uncertainty. Some of the significant uncertainties, and the information required to resolve them, are as follows:

1. The information for 2008 is both incomplete and unaudited. We would need to see a full, audited, annual report at least, and it is quite likely that we would need additional information about, for example, the age and condition of property, plant and equipment and inventory.

2. The only amount recognised separately in the financial statements in respect of the defined benefits pension scheme is the net liability. Many detailed disclosures are required by IAS 19, and we would need to scrutinise these carefully. The costs of the scheme are presumably recognised somewhere within the income statement, and their location could affect our analysis of the statements.

3. The associate has been turning in significant losses. We would need information about it in order to understand the group's involvement and continuing commitment.

4. If present trends continue the group could face insolvency before too long. There has been no dividend in the recent past, and return on equity, poor in 2007, is now negative. It would be necessary to know more about the principal shareholders and the extent to which they are likely to continue to support the business. It is possible that a takeover bid could be made for the business, and if we had lent significant amounts to the business, our relationship could be jeopardised.

5. The existing level of gearing is high, and as previously remarked, some of the borrowings fall due to be repaid within the short term. We would need to know a great deal more about the existing lenders, terms of loans and the nature and extent of security provided.

**Appendix – calculation of ratios**

|  | 2008 | 2007 |
|---|---|---|
| Return on capital employed* | (-4.9 + 5.4)/(141.9 + 57.2 + 28.7) = 0.2% | (1.1 +6.2)/(145.1 + 67.1 + 12.4) = 3.2% |
| Net margin | 0.5/256.3 = 0.2% | 7.3/281.7 = 2.6% |
| Gross margin | 29.7/256.3 = 11.6% | 38.6/281.7 = 13.7% |
| Asset turnover | 256.3/227.8 = 1.13 times | 281.7/224.6 = 1.25 times |
| Inventory turnover | 226.6/132.4 = 1.7 times | 243.1/125.6 = 1.9 times |
| Receivables days | (51.7 x 365)/256.3 = 73 days | (58.2 x 365)/281.7 = 75 days |
| Trade payables days** | (150.1 x 365)/226.6 = 242 days | (161.2 x 365)/243.1 = 242 days |
| Quick ratio | 51.7/178.8 = 0.29 | (58.2 + 4.8)/173.6 = 0.36 |
| Gearing ratio | (57.2 + 28.7)/227.8 = 37.7% | (67.1 + 12.4)/224.6 = 35.4% |

* Using equity plus borrowings (short and long term) as capital employed. Other alternatives would be acceptable.

** Using cost of sales as a proxy for purchases

# Suggested solutions

## 5  Question five

### 1.  Check exact requirements

We are asked, for ELB, to calculate ratios up to a maximum of 8 marks, analyse financial performance and financial position, and consider any other matters the Board of ELB would need to consider regarding the financing of the entity.

### 2.  Review of information provided

■ ELB has been pursuing expansionist policies. Sometimes this leads to poor cost control and liquidity problems.

■ ELB has revalued its PPE. This should be considered when computing accounting ratios for comparability purposes.

■ ELB has available-for-sale financial assets. For ratio analysis purposes this is equivalent to saying that these assets are revalued, as gains or losses on re-measurement are not recognised in profit and loss.

■ There is a large funding requirement in 2010 when the bonds become repayable. These bonds have loan covenants attaching to them.

### 3.  Review of the financial statements as a whole

■ There has been significant increase in PPE in the period, maybe in line with the expansion strategy. However some of the increase is caused by the revaluation.

■ Inventories have risen by 20%. This is more or less in line with the increase in revenue.

■ Trade receivables have decreased whilst revenues have increased. This must mean that the receivables days have decreased.

■ There has been a deterioration in the cash position from a net positive balance of 120 to short term borrowings of 270.

→

- Revenues have increased by around 20% but profits have fallen. It looks like this is caused by poor cost control.

## 4. Calculation of specific ratios required in the question

The ratios relevant to the debt covenant will be calculated and are included in the appendix to the report.

## 5. Calculation of other relevant ratios

Given the review we have already performed in step 3 profitability ratios seem particularly relevant. These are included in the table in the appendix to the report.

## 6. Specific observations

The ratios confirm the analysis already carried out. Profitability has declined overall due to poor cost control. The impact of the revaluation impacts on profitability as well as on gearing, which unsurprisingly has reduced. It is important to comment on the situation regarding the covenants.

## 7. Answer in report format

**(a) See Appendix**

**(b) Report on ELB**

The following report is based on the financial statements of ELB and refers to ratios that are calculated in Appendix A of this report.

### Financial performance

Revenue has increased by 18% since 2007 due to the aggressive expansion policy pursued in the last two years. It is encouraging that we have maintained the gross profit margin, which shows good control over cost of sales.

Profit before tax, however has dropped significantly from 17% to 13·3%. This is due to a 55% increase in distribution costs and administrative expenses in the year and increased finance costs. It is likely that the expansion policy has included marketing and that new distribution channels have been introduced to service the increased market share.

The interest cover has dropped from 11·9 to 9·8 and although this is still above the target of 9·5, the bank will be concerned about the falling margins and the effect this is having on the interest cover. Action should be taken to control administration and distribution costs in the coming period.

Return on capital employed has fallen from 19·5% to 14·6% due to decreased profit and increased capital employed. The ratio will have been affected by the revaluation of non-current assets in the year, which accounts for a significant part of the increased capital.

### Financial position

Gearing has decreased significantly from 68·7% to 48·6% in the year and has achieved the threshold set by the bank.

The long term debt has not however decreased in the year, instead this fall is due to increasing equity, resulting from the revaluation in the year, profit earned in the year and the gain recognised on available for sale investments. The gearing ratio, without the revaluation would be 56%.

The current ratio has dropped below the target level from 1·9 to 1·45 and the quick ratio has also dropped well below the target of 1·1 to 0·71. Cash held has decreased from a positive balance of $120,000 to an overdraft position of $270,000. In addition, trade payables at the year-end have increased and receivables days have fallen from 66 days to 46 days. Customers are being pressed for payment while it looks likely that the settlement of payables is being delayed. These issues indicate problems with working capital and are signs that the ELB are overtrading. It is important that we illustrate to the bank that we have a strategy in place for easing the pressure on working capital and are not expanding too quickly. It does appear that the bank has supported us to date as we did breach the covenants at last year's reporting date and it has still offered us the finance.

(c) I have noted below some additional points that may be considered for inclusion in the agenda:

- Identify sources of working capital – it is vital that we can illustrate to the bank that we are urgently seeking to improve working capital to support the expansion strategy.

- Bonds repayable – the bonds are due to be repaid in July 2010, which is likely to be 12-18 months from now, and not only do we need the cash to repay them, we also need to secure some longer term funding if we are to continue to trade and expand. The cost of that funding will have an impact on the interest cover, which is already close to the acceptable threshold set by the bank. The bonds currently

→

pay 6% and funding with a significantly higher associated cost is likely to decrease the interest cover further.

■ Working capital control - the current approach to managing working capital indicates that ELB is chasing for payment and delaying creditor payments and this cannot be sustained in the longer term as it is likely to damage relationships with customers and suppliers.

■ Sell investments – the available for sale investments performed well in the year and selling these investments could provide a good source of funding and would provide an immediate injection to working capital.

⑧

## Appendix A

| Ratios | 2008 $'000 | | 2007 $'000 | |
|---|---|---|---|---|
| Gearing (debt/ equity) | 11,400/ 23,460 | 48.6% | 11,200/ 16,300 | 68.7% |
| Gearing without revaluation | 11,400/ (23,460- 3,100) | 56% | | |
| Or: Gearing incl. overdraft | 11,670/ 23,460 | 49.7% | | |
| Interest cover (profit before interest/interest) | (4,560 + 520)/520 | 9.8 | (4,900 + 450)/450 | 11.9 |
| ROCE (profit before interest/ equity + long term debt) | (4,560 + 520)/ (23,460 + 11,400) | 14.6% | (4,900 + 450)/ (16,300 + 11,200) | 19.5% |
| GP % (GP/ turnover) | 10,200/ 34,200 | 29.8% | 8,650/ 28,900 | 29.9% |
| Profitability (profit for yr/ turnover) | 3,260/ 34,200 | 9.5% | 3,500/ 28,900 | 12.1% |
| Current ratio (CA/CL) | 8,800/ 6,070 | 1.45 | 8,920/ 4,700 | 1.9 |
| Quick ratio (CA – inventories/ CL) | (8,800 – 4,500)/ 6,070 | 0.71 | (8,920 - 3,600)/ 4,700 | 1.13 |
| Inventory turnover (Cost of sales/ inventory) | 24,000/ 4,500 | 5.3 times | 20,250/ 3,600 | 5.6 times |
| Receivables days (receivables x 365/turnover) | (4,300 x 365)/34,200 | 46 days | (5,200 x 365)/28,900 | 66 days |

# Suggested solutions

## 6 Question six

### 1. Checking of exact requirements

We are asked to prepare a report advising a shareholder in the RG group who has noticed that profitability has declined and is considering disposing of his shareholding. He refers to segment reports that are not actually provided. There is emphasis in the requirements on computing relevant ratios.

### 2. Read all the information provided

■ RG has made a significant investment in part of its business this year. The benefits appear likely to flow through next year and beyond.

■ The above issue appears key here because the client appears to be basing a desire to sell on decreased profits since last year. We must be aware of the possibility of an upturn should the new investment be successful.

### 3. Review the financial statements

■ Revenues are fairly static but it looks like gross margins have improved slightly.

■ Other operating costs have risen significantly and this is a weakness that needs referring to. Administrative expenses are reduced by profits on the disposal of investments that will include recycled gains recognised in other comprehensive income (or equity) in previous periods. Therefore the 'true' increase in administrative expenses may be higher than this.

■ RG has invested in an associate during the period.

■ There is a significant increase in inventory and receivables. Some increase would be expected given the expansion but the percentage increase looks very large indeed.

■ There has been a substantial sale of investments and it appears that at least some of the proceeds are being used to pay off borrowings.

## 4. Compute the ratios required in the question

In this case this step is not required.

## 5. Compute relevant ratios to assist with the analysis

In this case profit margin and asset utilisation ratios seem the most appropriate. Computations are included in the appendix to the suggested answer that appears below.

## 6. Specific observations

Profitability and asset utilisation (as measured by the inventory and receivables ratios) have fallen but this could be caused by the stated expansion policy. In situations where the business is growing ratios that include a period number (like profit) and a 'point of time' number like capital employed, need to be interpreted with caution.

(a) **Report to**

Subject RG Group – financials 30 June 2009

**Profitability**

Revenue has remained static over the last 12 months and yet distribution costs and admin expenses have increased significantly. The cost incurred in setting up the new distribution channels and the employment and training of the new sales team, however, would be expected to increase revenue in the forthcoming period as activity has just recently started in these areas – this can be seen by the fact that June 2009 orders are higher than expected. A positive point is that there is a slight increase in gross profit margin from 25.3% to 26.7%. It will be important that this is maintained in new market sales.

Administrative expenses have increased significantly since last year from $22m to $37m while revenue has remained constant. Although some of this may be related to the setting up of new sales channels, the increase is masked slightly by the gain on the sale of the available for sale investment of $4m which has been netted off the expenses. Removing this would result in administrative expenses increasing from $22m to $41m in the year, which indicates a lack of management control over costs. This is a major contributor to the fall in net profit from 10.6% to 7.8%. In addition, the 2009 profit for the period includes the share of profit of associate of $5m. Without the associate the profit percentage for 2009 falls to just 6.9%.

It is imperative that the management now turn their attention to the control of costs to ensure that the expansion in markets brings appropriate net returns.

On a more positive note the management appear to be making good investment decisions in respect of both the financial assets that they have sold and those that they have retained (with gains taken to equity in the period of $6m). The investment in the associate has also brought $5m which has helped the bottom line profit. We do not know when during the year the associate was acquired therefore it is possible that the associate's return could be even greater next year. Finance costs have been kept to a minimum and interest cover is more than adequate at this time.

**Efficiency**

The return on capital employed has fallen and is generally at quite a low level. This may be due to the fact that significant investment was made in 2009 and the revenues of this investment have not yet been earned. This return would be expected to increase in the next period.

Payables days have remained relatively constant, however the receivables days have increased from 48 days to 69 days which again is an indication that management need to tighten up control. The cash balance has dropped significantly due to the payment of the dividend and the repayment of the loan and so it is essential that receivables days are reduced to boost the cash balance and prevent the company having to go into overdraft. In addition, with the new markets being targeted, RG may have to offer incentives to new customers and so tight control of existing accounts and control of all new receivables should be a priority going forward.

Inventory days have increased from 70 days to 115 days. Since revenue has remained steady, this looks like RG is preparing to meet the orders from the new markets. This would be expected to return to a steady level once the level of regular orders is established.

The current ratio has decreased slightly but it still provides adequate cover for current liabilities, however since inventories have increased the quick ratio will provide a more accurate picture. The quick ratio has fallen from 2.1 to 1.14. This is due to the increase in receivables and the fall in the cash balance due to the payment of the dividend and the repayment of the loan.

**Financial position**

The gearing ratio is low and has in fact fallen from 43% to 30% due to the repayment of part of the loan and the share issue in the period.

It appears that the low returns are temporary and that the investments made in an effort to increase market share are likely to bring future benefits. Although RG needs to regain tighter control of receivables and expenses, the management appear to have made good decisions on investments and have shown good management of working capital up to now. The finance providers clearly believe RG to be low risk as the long term borrowings carry an interest rate of less than 4%. The shareholders have continued to support the entity via the share issue in the period and appear to have been compensated for the lack of growth by the receipt of a dividend, even though it is not covered by the earnings.

It looks like prospects are good for RG.

## Appendix I - Ratio calculations

| | 2009 | 2008 |
|---|---|---|
| ROCE | ($60m + $6m)/ ($515m + $154m) = 9.9% | ($75m + $8m)/ ($475m + $205m) = 12.2% |
| Gross profit | $154m/$576m = 26.7% | $145m/$573m = 25.3% |
| Net profit | $45m/$576m = 7.8% | $61m/$573m = 10.6% |
| Net profit without associate | $40m/$576m = 6.9% | |
| Asset turnover | $576m/$669m = 0.9 times | $573m/$680m = 9.0 times |
| Inventory days | $133m x 365/$422m = 115 days | $82m x 365/$428m = 70 days |
| Receivables days | $109m/$576m x 365 days = 69 days | $76m/$573m x 365 days = 48 days |
| Payables days | $91m/$422m x 365 days = 79 days | $87m/$428m x 365 days = 74 days |

# Suggested solutions

## 7 Question seven

### 1. Checking exact requirements of the question

We are asked to prepare a report that evaluates the suitability of a target company (CAD) for acquisition and reflect on the increasing tendency towards non-financial corporate reporting.

### 2. Reading of the whole question and considering the implications for financial analysis

■ CAD is a company that develops environmentally friendly products that are of potential benefit to BCA.

■ In common with many companies of this type, CAD has few tangible assets and therefore finds it difficult to raise finance due to lack of security.

■ The Chief Scientific Officer (CSO) is a key employee of CAD and were she to leave CAD this would severely curtail its effectiveness.

### 3. Review of financial information contained within the question

■ Revenues have increased significantly but profits have fallen. There is clearly a problem with costs. In situations where costs are significant there is always the possibility that they have been inappropriately capitalised.

■ The statement of financial position shows a significant increase in intangible assets. We would need to know exactly what these assets were so that we could assess their validity.

■ It appears that inventory and receivables have increased by more than the year on year percentage increase in revenues. This could be partly caused by the rapid expansion of the business and the consequential effect on ratios that compare 'point of time' amounts with 'period' amounts.

→

■ There has been a significant reduction in cash and cash equivalents and an increase in short term borrowings. Financially, the business looks somewhat unstable.

4. Calculation of ratios specifically required in the question

Not required here.

5. Calculation of ratios relevant to the analysis

These are contained in an appendix to the report. The calculations have focused on margins and asset utilisation as these appear to be the major issues with the business.

6. Appraisal of information and ratios

The decrease in gross margin compared with the increased revenues could be caused by the large development costs and the bonus paid to the CSO.

Other operating expenses as a %age of sales have actually fallen when you compare the gross and net margins. This shows satisfactory control of such expenses.

Financing (or lack of it) is a key issue for this business. Their debt collection is poor, maybe due to the focus on expansion.

The business may well be a good target for an acquirer with funds to invest, but care would need to be taken to preserve the expertise of the CSO for the business.

## (a) Preliminary report to Board

Subject: Potential acquisition of CAD

### Profitability

The gross margin achieved by CAD has dropped significantly from 21% last year to 14.5% (see appendix 1 for ratios). This is likely to be due to the cost of the new technology and the bonus paid to the Chief Scientific Officer (CSO). Sales are up 22% and indications are that future periods will see further revenue increases due to the development of the new technology. The main challenge for CAD will be staying in business long enough to take advantage of these further revenues. We would have to consider if these future contracts might be compromised if we were to acquire CAD, as they may trade with our competitors. The net profit margin is down slightly from 3.5% to 2.5% due mainly to the finance costs incurred in 2009. The net profit fall is less than that of gross profit and indicates that other costs and expenses have been well controlled.

### Efficiency

The receivables days are crippling the flow of cash in the business. The recovery of amounts due has risen from 60 days to 92 days. CAD's main challenge is dealing with large customers with a significant outstanding balance and may not have the credit control resources to manage these accounts or are not in a position to successfully negotiate because of size and relative dependency. If, however, BCA was to takeover CAD and implemented stricter credit control procedures then this could be eradicated. Cutting this back to 60 days would release more than $300,000 and would remove the need to rely on expensive short term funding.

The interest paid in 2009 is at approximately 10%. That is likely to be because CAD cannot offer the bank substantial amounts of tangible non-current assets on which security can be taken. This is likely to be less of an issue for BCA as we are an established multinational and would be able to secure funding at more competitive rates if required.

In addition, it is likely that CAD is unable to successfully negotiate with its customers for early payment as the contracts are all with large established companies, however again that may not be an issue if contracts were negotiated by BCA.

Payables looks high, however the payables days has stayed relatively static in the 60s and suppliers have continued to supply as inventories have increased so the delay in settlement seems not to be a problem. BCA may choose to reduce the payables level to avoid any negative impact on its credit rating.

### Potential target entity

CAD appears to be a sound investment provided the future services of the CSO can be secured. CAD shareholders are willing to surrender control if the company's future and their own is secure. The business is profitable and future prospects look positive. The contracts that CAD has are with established companies and there appears to be an order book to provide future services for the next couple of years at least. The issues of funding and debt collection are likely to be able to be solved by BCA. The key personnel member appears to have been well tied into the business and so the current management team clearly know what is vital to the survival of their business.

(b) (i)    It has been recognised that financial statements report historical events and transactions and are generally backward looking. They are therefore often of limited use to users that are focused on the entity's future prospects and potential results. It is generally agreed that the relevance of financial information would be improved if some information about the entity's future objectives and challenges and the strategies in place to overcome those challenges was included. Information on the dynamics and risks of the entity would also be useful – e.g. reliance on key personnel or development of technology. However this information cannot be audited and therefore lacks reliability which is a key qualitative characteristic of financial statements.

This has led to the growth in narrative reporting in corporate reports. The entity should give a balanced report on the activities and performance of the period and expected performance for the immediate future and in turn shareholders must recognise that this information does not have the added comfort of an audit opinion.

(ii)   An OFR type report would be helpful to potential investors in CAD as the financial statements do not provide the information that is key to this type of high-tech industry. The low levels of tangible non-current asset make it pointless to calculate traditional ratios like return on capital employed and so comparisons with other potential investments are restricted. It also makes it hard for these entities to raise external finance as there are few assets available as security. This is an example of where the value of the business lies in the intellectual property within the entity through the patents and the know-how and technical expertise of the staff.

However the key elements in the future viability of the entity lie in the patents and key personnel and the contracts – much of which is absent from the historical financial statements. A management commentary on these areas would be invaluable to investors and other lenders as it would help them understand the underlying business.

The relationships with the CSO would also be discussed under the risks and relationships section as losing the technical developer would have a significant effect on the long term prospects of the entity. The high receivables would also be explained and would enable the entity to explain the details of arrangements as some readers would assume, in the absence of any information to the contrary, that it is as a result of poor credit control.

A narrative report would give the management the opportunity to explain the dynamics of the business and the investment in future technological improvements that are not evident from the numerical information presented in the financial statements.

## Appendix - ratios

| | | |
|---|---|---|
| Receivables days | $1,091K/$4,330K x 365 days = 92 days | $587K/$3,562K x 365 days = 60 days |
| Payables days | $687K/$3,702K x 365 days = 68 days | $485K/$2,810K x 365 days = 63 days |
| Finance costs – approximate rate | $13K/$123K = 10.6% | |
| Gross profit | $628K/$4,330K x 100 = 14.5% | $752K/$3,562K x 100 = 21% |
| Net profit | $108K/$4,330K x 100 = 2.5% | $125/$3,562K x 100 = 3.5% |

# Index

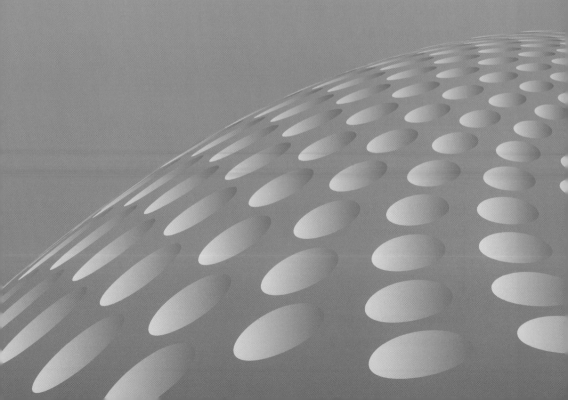

# A

## Q

## R

## S

## T

## W